ORIGINAL PRAYER

ORIGINAL PRAYER

Themes from the Christian tradition

Lavinia Byrne

First published in Great Britain in 2008

Society for Promoting Christian Knowledge
36 Causton Street
London SW1P 4ST

British Library Cataloguing-in-Publication Data
A catalogue record for this book is available from the British Library

ISBN 978–0–281–05999–7

1 3 5 7 9 10 8 6 4 2

Typeset by Graphicraft Ltd, Hong Kong
Printed in Great Britain by Ashford Colour Press

Produced on paper from sustainable forests

This book is dedicated to Professor Steven Gill MB, BS, MS, FRCS, Karen O'Sullivan CNS and the team at the Department of Neurosurgery, Frenchay Hospital, Bristol – for reasons which will become apparent.

Contents

Introduction

Prayer is a state of being before God. Long before it becomes a conscious activity – something we do – it already exists as a necessary condition of inner attentiveness. The Christian tradition teaches us that we are made by God. Our Creator calls us into conversation; or at least to attentive silence, so that we can listen. This relationship does not have to be negotiated; it is a given, and in turning to God in prayer we do no more than give expression to this primary relationship.

Prayer is not our work. It is something the Holy Spirit does in us, opening our hearts and minds and raising them to the Father. We pray in Christ, uniting our prayers with the prayers of Jesus.

This book offers various themes from the Christian tradition to help you to pray. Its title makes a play on words, for original prayer is prayer that looks to its roots. So Chapters 1–4 look consciously at great historical figures from the Christian story. Teresa of Avila takes us to medieval Spain and visions of growth in prayer that are strikingly contemporary in their psychological astuteness. With Francis of Assisi we learn to put God at the centre of everything and to let go of worldly ambition, finding true simplicity and contentment. Benedict takes us to the monastery as a 'school for the Lord's service', a place where we can learn how to live and pray in an organic way. Ignatius of Loyola teaches us to 'seek and find God in all things' and to discern the will of God in all our activities.

Treasures from the Orthodox tradition come to us through the 'Jesus Prayer' (Chapter 5), as timeless as history itself. The theme of pilgrimage and prayer is taken up by Chapter 6, while music and art (Chapters 7 and 8) too have a contribution to make and we learn to use both when coming into the presence of God. Then there is Chapter 9 about online prayer and the book's title is given fresh force. For prayer is capable of re-inventing itself and adapting even to the most modern of our media. Go online and find access to God in a screenful of megabytes. The final chapter retreats from cyberspace and faces the really difficult question of how we pray when we are ill. Jesus said, 'I am the resurrection and the life' (John 11.25). How do we prepare ourselves to face eternal life?

At the end of each chapter you will find practical exercises. These are intended to help you as you pray and to lead you to fresh and original ways of renewing your own spiritual and personal life of faith.

1

Teresa of Avila and Carmelite prayer

Teresa: a woman of her times

Teresa of Avila was a revolutionary. She lived in tumultuous times and her life was turned around by her relationship with God. So her story is about a journey in the spiritual life and that is why it makes a good starting point for this book. For Teresa understood that the life of prayer is about taking risks and change and growth, rather than standing still. She invites us to discover prayer as a vocation, a calling from God, and she shows how we can answer this call by writing about herself and her times.

The story begins in 1515 when Teresa Sanchez de Cepeda y Ahumada was born at Avila in Spain. This was a tricky time in European history, with new relationships forming between the followers of Islam and of Christianity and divisions developing between different kinds of Christian. Twenty-two years earlier the Moors or Muslims had been expelled from Spain by Ferdinand of Aragon and his wife, Isabella of Castile; two years later a monk called Martin Luther would pin his 95 Theses to a church door in Wittenberg, triggering the Protestant Reformation in Germany. Ordinary people in everyday society and Church leaders alike struggled to find a new identity for life in contemporary Europe.

A brand new world had opened up too with the discovery of the Americas in 1492 and the old certainties no longer held the promise they had had for the little girl's ancestors. Except that this is not true. For in 1947 an article was published that told us something about Teresa's parentage that had been unknown until then, namely that she carried Jewish blood on her father's side. In sixteenth-century Spain, to be associated with the Jewish community would have been considered shameful, as the Catholic townsfolk of Avila saw them as enemies. After all, the Jews had conspired to kill Jesus, or so the wisdom of the time went. For Teresa's family this was a dishonourable secret because her father had been a *converso*, a forced convert to Catholicism in Toledo, where they lived before moving to Avila. Her older brother could even remember seeing his father being beaten with whips and made to take part in a public penitential procession around the churches of Toledo. The shame became a terrible family secret and one to be skirted around at all costs.

Not only were Jews to be shunned but all traces of Islam too had been rubbed out. When the Moors were expelled from the walled city of Avila, the whole nature of that part of southern Castile changed. For the Muslims had been a benign influence. Their architecture, with its walled courtyards and musical water fountains, had been built by an industrious community of craftsmen and women who valued working with leather, enamels, jewels and silk. The Moors, as they were called, had discovered algebra, the number zero and gave us the word 'alcohol', and brought the life of the east to the west. The Jews too, with their banking and financial skills, had made the city prosperous, and in 1492 more than eleven thousand of them were evicted from Avila alone, more than half the city's population.

Teresa was her father's sixth child. His first wife had died after giving birth to the first three and his second died when Teresa was still young. The Ahumada home was a devout one, with daily mass and family prayers, and we would know little of her early life were it not for the fact that she chose to record an adventurous episode from it. In 1522, when she was seven, she persuaded her brother Rodrigo to run away from home with her, on a mission to convert the Moors. She understood them to be the enemies of true religion and enemies of Spain, and set off for the *tierra de moros* or North Africa. Half a mile from home the pair were waylaid by their uncle Francisco and brought back to safety.

Where had the young Teresa found the inspiration for this journey? From books. There were many lives of the saints in the family home and she read these avidly, looking for inspiration. She would build little huts in the garden and pretend to be a hermit. When her mother died, the little girl was 13 and three years later she was sent off to school at an Augustinian convent called Our Lady of Grace.

At 21 she ran away from home again, to join the Carmelite sisters. Their Convent of the Incarnation in Avila housed some 180 nuns and Teresa embraced their way of life with enthusiasm. She had two rooms, with a staircase joining the downstairs oratory to an upstairs bedroom. The full rule of the Carmelites was not observed particularly strictly and Teresa had friends in the community who gave her emotional stability and encouragement. She enjoyed a game of chess and would dance to the sound of the tambourine along with the more usual disciplines of convent life, such as prayer and fasting.

For all that she eventually fell ill and had to go to stay with her sister Maria and brother-in-law, Martin Guzman, who lived in a village called Becedas. On the way there she stayed over with her uncle Pedro in Ortigosa, where a wise friend of his lent her a book called *The Third Spiritual Alphabet*. This came as a revelation. It spoke to her desire for union with God and suggested that praying meant more than simply saying the words of prayers over and over. Rather she was encouraged to let her mind run with ideas, to think, to meditate and to enquire of God.

On her return to the convent her health improved and she reflected on what she had learnt. Change came gradually over the years, including the massive change that would give her the courage and energy to reform the Carmelite Order and to make a host of new foundations where the rule would be followed more strictly.

For a long time though, she had trouble praying and decided to give up on any experiments with it. So the middle years of her life at the Convent of the Incarnation were not particularly fruitful. Only when her father died in 1544 did she confess her problems to a priest and receive help and support. She began to pray again and found the inspiration to embark on the second part of what would be a much more varied and also frenetic life.

In all she founded 16 new convents, travelling the length and breadth of Spain on her enterprises. She wrote extensively, sending copious letters – which she could write with both hands at once – to her many friends and to the priests who guided and directed her. She wrote books describing the spiritual life and the work of God as she experienced it. Best of all she left following generations with inspiration and powerful images to illuminate what became her teachings. Teresa of Avila died in 1582 at the age of 67, after years of devout service of God and a colourful life. She was canonized in 1622 and made a doctor of the Church in 1970, the first woman saint ever to receive this honour.

What did Teresa teach?

Teresa of Avila's greatest teaching was about prayer. She looked at her own life reflectively and began to make connections about how God works with individuals. Her deepest desire was for union with God, but she learnt the hard way that this did not come about by magic, through some effort of the will. If anything it was only when she stopped trying so hard that God could take over and her life become one of grace.

One of her most telling images explains how the life of faith and prayer develops within an individual. She chooses a picture that belongs to the parched land of her childhood, the sun-dried soil of Castile. So she speaks of a garden and how the innermost being of a plant or a person can only grow with watering. That is how it is with prayer, she argues. At first we make a great effort all by ourselves, drawing water from a well, as it were, and heaving it about laboriously by our own efforts. Then we learn how to set up systems, so we use waterwheels and buckets which will do the heavy grind for us, but still ensure that we continue to grow. Where there is a stream in the garden though, something new begins to happen. God is actively at work, meandering through our days and watering our souls with graces that make their way to us without effort on our part. But best of all is rain, where we abandon ourselves to refreshment from above and all is grace.

Simple imagery, but a nice description of human striving and where it ends most restfully. The point is that God needs co-operation from the human soul. That part of ourselves which seeks God needs to be taken care of so that it can become more receptive. Any gardener knows the importance of preparation work to ensure that the soil in a garden is at its best for the first sowing of the year and the early spring watering.

What is telling in Teresa's writings is her insistence on God's work in our lives. Ultimately all spiritual gifts come from him, including the grace to work for change in the world. Part of her book *The Way of Perfection* is an extended reflection on the Lord's Prayer, offering inspiration in the form of a commentary. This gives us a sense of how Teresa herself first learnt to pray, how she allowed her mind to come to understanding by letting it savour the words she was using. Even the most familiar of words, such as those of a well-loved prayer, she argues, can open out and blossom when they are used for spiritual reflection in this way.

In 1577 she wrote what is arguably her greatest work. *The Interior Castle* tells the awesome story of the journey of the soul. This is the mature Teresa sharing her insights and the full wisdom of her journey in prayer. She sees a castle in her imagination, with different rooms that lead through into a central chamber where God lives and union with God is realized. The first of these rooms or mansions is about the drama of self-discovery and self-knowledge. The soul becomes alert to the possibility of journeying. This is a crucial moment, for it leads to the question: where is this journey to be made? For the first 20 years of her life Teresa had lived on the outside of herself, assuming that the spiritual life was about journeying towards some distant goal. The childhood experience of looking for Moors to convert in some remote land was always a powerful metaphor in her life. Only in her middle years did Teresa come to understand that the truest journey is the one we make towards the core of our very own being.

To realize this is to come to the second mansion, to be lit up by the desire for prayer and conversation with God. This means a kind of conversion, a turning about on ourselves so that we begin to face inwards rather than outwards. Christ is revealed to us and seeks us out, leading us towards the third mansion, where we are called to a life of virtue. Teresa now notes that many people live their entire spiritual lives at this point. They get stuck in the third mansion, which, while being a wholly admirable place, is nevertheless quite comfortable. It is a place of virtue and many virtuous people become complacent. They fail to take the risk of another journey. Yet the fourth mansion beckons. It is a place of transition, for here human effort becomes transformed by God's grace. God takes over the life of the soul, just as, in her earlier example, the stream in the dry garden takes over the work of the water carrier or our own irrigation systems. The prayerful person now moves from a spiritual life based less on effort and action to one based more on receptivity. Prayer becomes more passive: the work of God, and not our own.

In the fifth mansion the soul feels as though it is asleep, enjoying the prayer of passive recollection, a sweet openness to the will of God and tender rest. There is a death, and it is the death of understanding which now surrenders itself into the understanding of God. Here she uses the image of a silkworm, and the way it grows through changing often. This is among the most memorable of any of the metaphors she uses, and it prepares us for life in the next mansion. For the sixth mansion too brings a kind of death with it, as here the will lets go and the soul is besieged by raptures, ecstasies and trances. Teresa writes from her own experience, so she tries to reassure the prayerful person that these spiritual phenomena, while unusual, are not totally terrifying. She teaches discernment, how to tell what is true from what is false, how to be led towards God and away from the sources of evil. All is gift and grace as the soul makes its way towards the innermost mansion of all, the place of true encounter and union with God. Here in the seventh mansion there is a strange forgetfulness of all that went before. The death or release of memory secures the presence of the soul in God, God in the soul.

A great mystic and a practical woman

Teresa's teaching on mysticism is so well developed that anyone interested in her message could be forgiven for thinking that there is no more to be said about her. Even the religious order she reformed so successfully is one of the Church's most hidden treasures, where Carmelite sisters and brothers pray for the world from behind the relative safety and obscurity of their convent walls. Only when the TV cameras penetrate do we get a rare glimpse of what goes on there. So why is she important for the rest of us too? What is her relevance for today's world?

I have an unusual way in which to examine her heritage, for the Roman Catholic parish church at my home in Wells in Somerset is a former Carmelite convent. The sisters left the place in the 1990s. The church is an odd shape, with an L-shaped chapel off it, facing the main altar. This is where the sisters used to kneel and pray. During Mass they received communion from the priest by approaching the grill or barrier that prevented people in the main body of the church from seeing them. As a child, I could hear their singing, a muffled sound of disembodied voices, and now I often choose to go to Mass in their part of the church. What strikes me most is the view they would have had. They would have been able to hear the service, obviously, but when they looked up, they would have seen an immense crucifix on the wall opposite, and above that a plain leaded window. That formed their total view.

So I pick up two messages about their spirituality: that it was focused on the person of Christ and that it came unadorned. For the rest of the congregation, in the body of the church, there is a totally different stained-glass window behind the main altar: one that is much more colourful, with a more obvious story to tell. It shows the Virgin Mary pictured in glory, as described in Revelation 12.1: 'A great portent appeared in heaven: a woman clothed with the sun, with the moon under her feet, and on her head a crown of twelve stars.' This representation is known to Catholic piety as Our Lady of Mount Carmel because it is how she was seen in a vision granted to an English Carmelite, St Simon Stock, who saw her depicted like this in Cambridge in 1251.

To her right are St John of the Cross, another Carmelite and friend and colleague of Teresa, along with St Joseph, representing great male praying saints. To Mary's left is St Teresa herself, along with St Francis Xavier. I should add that the parents of a young Carmelite nun in the community, called Sister Francis Xavier, endowed the church. But whereas the sisters themselves could not have seen this window, the message for those of us in the body of the church is clear: contemplative prayer is there for women and men alike and not simply for the sisters behind their grill, whose life was dedicated to the pursuit of it.

The great convent itself has now been converted into flats and there are two houses built in the former grounds or garden of the convent. Would it be fanciful to say that a benign spirit prevails around the place because of the prayerful lives of its former occupants? By the 1950s and 1960s, when I was a child, only one of the nuns was known by name to the local people, because only one of them ever came out of her enclosure. She was the Out Sister, whose task it was to shop for the rest of the community and to negotiate their life in the outer world. I remember seeing her with an immense basket, waiting patiently at the off-licence for the priest's tobacco and whisky, or at the fish queue for the latest catch. I admired her for being visible and she had the advantage of being tall, as well as of her distinctive habit.

What I now realize I was seeing was an immensely practical and capable woman, another Teresa in fact. The handle Teresa usually bears is that of mystic and contemplative, but there is another side to her character which makes her very much a saint for our own times. She had a good head for figures and for business because her concerns were increasingly with the reform of the Carmelite order.

Many of her letters show how busy she became as the real work of her life took her over, namely the many foundations she undertook. Put in concrete terms this meant buying property, often in remote places, and equipping communities with all they would need to get going and to survive. She had to worry about money and business dealings, about legal transactions and property speculation.

For her there was nothing soppy or disengaged about prayer. As she wrote in *The Interior Castle*,

> When I see people very diligently trying to discover what kind of prayer they are experiencing and so completely wrapped up in their prayers that they seem afraid to stir, or to indulge in a moment's thought, lest they should lose the slightest degree of

> the tenderness and devotion which they had been feeling, I realise how little they understand of the road to the attainment of union. They think that the whole thing consists in this. But no, sisters, no; what the Lord desires is works. (5, 3, 12)

And by works she meant just that: hard work, cracking on with things, not being too disembodied or refined to worry about practicalities. For a flavour of her ability to engage with reality, how about this extract from one of her letters?

> Jesus be with you. I said in the letter that went with the Alba courier that the sardines had arrived in good condition and that the sweets had duly arrived too, though I had rather you had kept the best ones. May God reward you.
>
> It is well with us both just now. What great things the Lord is doing! He seems to be pleased to show forth his greatness in raising up wretched creatures and doing us all these favours – and I know of none more wretched than you and I. I must tell you that, for over a week, I have been in such a condition that, if I were to go on, I should hardly be able to attend to all my business. Since I wrote to you I have had the raptures again, and they have been most distressing. Several times I have had them in public – during Matins, for example. It is useless to resist them and they are impossible to conceal. I get so dreadfully ashamed that I feel I want to hide away somewhere. I pray God earnestly not to let them happen to me in public: will you make this prayer for me too, for it is an extremely awkward thing and I don't believe my prayer is any better for it? Latterly I have been going about almost as if I were drunk; but at least it is clear that the soul is well employed, for, as the faculties are not free, it is a grievous thing for the soul to have to occupy itself with anything save the object of its desire.
>
> Previously, for nearly a week, I have been in such a state that I could hardly think a single good thought, so severely was I suffering from aridity. (*The Letters of Saint Teresa*, vol. I)

Raptures and aridity; sardines and sweets. The mixture is as intoxicating to read about as it evidently was to experience. So what kept Teresa going? What was her anchor throughout all these different experiences?

The person of Christ, whom she described as 'this centre of the soul'. He was her living Lord who did great things for her and to whom she was bound by love, by detachment from earthly things and by humility. These attitudes are counter-cultural because nowadays we live in a society that is inclined to value people for what they have and what they achieve. Teresa was not against achievement but rather she wanted it bound about with humility so that high achievers could always be looking to praise God rather than themselves.

This is a very simple message about putting God and other people first. At one time it was at the heart of Christian asceticism because it drove the saints to be selfless. In our own times it has become extremely counter-cultural because we live in a world of fragile egos where people question the value of living for others. Teresa of Avila has a message for us because her spirituality was robust and it made her robust enough to value other people and their good more than her own.

The Carmelite charism

Unlike most other religious communities, the Carmelite Order has no named founder. For inspiration it looked to the life of the prophet Elijah, whose encounter with God on Mount Carmel is described in 1 Kings 19.11–12.

> He said, 'Go out and stand on the mountain before the LORD, for the LORD is about to pass by.' Now there was a great wind, so strong that it was splitting mountains and breaking rocks in pieces before the LORD, but the LORD was not in the wind; and after the wind an earthquake, but the LORD was not in the earthquake; and after the earthquake a fire, but the LORD was not in the fire; and after the fire a sound of sheer silence. When Elijah heard it, he wrapped his face in his mantle and went out and stood at the entrance of the cave.

The order's origins can be dated to the end of the twelfth and early thirteenth centuries, when a group of nameless hermits gathered beside the well of Elijah on Mount Carmel, hoping to repeat his experience. They wanted to follow Christ together and asked the Patriarch of Jerusalem, St Albert, to write a *Rule* or way of life for them to follow. He used ideas that had been helpful to previous hermits and added inspirations of his own. The result was a document that emphasized brotherly (and later) sisterly love and service of others as expressions of following the person of Jesus (to see the *Rule*, go to <http://carmelites.org/source> or <http://carmelnet.org/chas/rule.htm>). Because prayer is an opening up to the ultimate mysteries, the earliest Carmelites saw prayer as the best way of giving true service to the world. Albert wrote,

> Each of you is to stay in his own cell or nearby, pondering the Lord's law by day and night and keeping watch at his prayers unless attending to some other duties. (*Rule*, verse 8)

The early hermits put prayer and contemplation of God at the heart of their way of life and of their service of God's world. By the time Teresa of Avila joined their number the purity of the Carmelite nuns' original call and its expression in a very simple lifestyle had dissipated. After all, theirs is no run of the mill existence and so some of its inspiration had gone precisely because it had become mundane, worldly, losing its cutting edge. By the sixteenth century, when Teresa first joined the community, it had become a place to park unmarried daughters so that they could enjoy a rather spoilt, if devout, existence. As we have seen, in the community Teresa joined at the Convent of the Incarnation in Avila, there were some 180 sisters, a number that she later realized made the dream unliveable.

So small was to be beautiful in her understanding, and she elected to set up communities of no more than 13 members. In the former Wells Carmel you can see the place where the turn used to be, namely the wooden swinging turnstile that visitors, along with postmen and milkmen, used to use to drop by things the community needed. Inside the house was spacious but simple and the upstairs rooms where the sisters lived are small, like servants' quarters. You can easily imagine them living within the plain whitewashed walls and see the sisters moving silently up and down the stripped pine stairs. Silence would be an important feature of a Carmelite day as silence enables the voice of God to be heard. St Albert wrote in the spirit of Psalm 62.5, 'For God alone my soul waits in silence, for my hope is from him', when he began his *Rule* with an exhortation to silence. For this reason Carmelites make a point of practising disciplines that encourage silence because silence leads to prayer. By today's standards, a Carmelite house would be a very quiet house.

Now Teresa was practical. She knew that true silence takes practice and that it is as much an inner as an outer attitude. Her contention was that the inner and the outer lives need each other. Indeed, the inner life has to be cultivated and this takes time, so by practising silence, the sisters would learn silence. The Carmelite sisters I heard singing from their chapel when I was a child made a sound that was far from musical. No one would join a monastery or convent for its choir or its way of approaching Gregorian chant, for instance. The sound was thin and childlike, stripped of all aspirations or pretensions and focused on God.

How can these qualities of simplicity and silence inspire us today? They seem to be so far away from the barrage of sound with which most of us surround ourselves. And because much of our sound is generated electronically, this means that we are surrounded by the possessions which make all this music and speech possible. Time too is at a premium. Many people are cash-rich and time-poor, and yet all may hear Teresa encouraging us to take God's call seriously; to free up some time and space for prayer; and to serve the world by contemplating the gift of God, the gift that is God, beyond all our possessions.

Ours is an anxious, troubled world and, astonishingly, we are still living with the results of fault lines that were etched on European culture and consciousness in sixteenth-century Spain when the Moors and Jews were first made unwelcome and chased off the map. Yet it is precisely from this, apparently remote, world that we are offered a vision of human living that values religious renewal first, seeing it not as a flight into extremism and fundamentalism, but rather as a rediscovery of what matters most, putting God at the heart of all we are and say and do. Is that the way out of contemporary political and religious conflict nowadays as well? For what we are offered by examining the life of Teresa of Avila is a mirror into which we can all gaze. The mirror is formed by a great pool of water. As we fall silent and as the ripples fade, we see ourselves more clearly and also, she believed, beyond all the imaging and imagining, we begin to gaze on God.

Some exercises to help you pray in the spirit of Teresa of Avila

1 'Prayer, in my view, is nothing but an intimate sharing between friends, being often alone with Him who we know loves us' (Teresa of Avila, *Life*, 8, 5).

Find a way of being alone, sit or kneel, close your eyes and take time to quieten yourself. Become aware of your mood. Place any worries or concerns before the Father. Ask the Holy Spirit to open your mind and heart to hear what God has to say to you. Listen to the words of Jesus: 'Peace I leave with you; my peace I give to you' (John 14.27).

2 Create a pool of silence by having a 'sound-fast'. Go round your house turning off all the TVs, radios and other sound systems. Then listen to the other sounds that normally you don't hear. If you can, go out of doors as well and see if you can hear any birdsong or natural sounds above the noise of traffic, planes, children playing and so on. Consciously

locate the quietest place possible and stand or sit in it for as long as you feel comfortable. Listen to yourself and notice what you feel. Try to repeat this exercise by revisiting this place and this experience for quick 'sound-free' moments and enjoy the benefits you begin to find there. This place can become your personal 'Carmel'.

3 Write out these words from Teresa and carry them round with you:

> Christ has no body now on earth but ours,
> no hands but ours, no feet but ours.
> Ours are the eyes through which must look out
> Christ's compassion on the world.
> Ours are the feet with which He is to go about doing good.
> Ours are the hands with which He blesses now.
>
> (St Teresa's Breastplate)

2

Francis of Assisi and a new lifestyle

The medieval burgher's son

Teresa of Avila inserted two key virtues into her turbulent world: silence and reform. She wanted to help people to pray and to come close to God, and she saw that they would grow and change as God took over their lives. Francis of Assisi was another radical. He too saw the need for virtuous people to be able to flourish, and the choices he saw as critical were to affect not simply the way he prayed, but what we would call his lifestyle as well. So Christian spirituality, as seen through the lens offered us by the life of Francis, is all about choices that affect the way we live.

His story has often been told because it is such an attractive and dramatic one. He was a rich merchant's son, born in Assisi in Umbria in 1182. We have a visual record of his world because the great thirteenth-century fresco artist, Giotto, painted his life story on the walls of the Upper Church in Assisi after Francis died. The fresco represents the most famous scenes from his life and acts as a kind of slide show, telling us his story against a vast backdrop populated by poor people and popes, saints and kings. For another view of what life was like in a bustling Italian city, the mural of Good Governance painted by Ambrogio Lorenzetti in Siena gives a series of vibrant street scenes. A shepherd herds his sheep through the city centre, a cobbler plies his trade in his shopfront, there is food and wine in abundance. As in Giotto's pictures, all the signs of prosperity are here, for Italy in the twelfth century was enjoying all the benefits of trade and was already poised on the brink of what would become the Renaissance.

Francis' father, a cloth merchant, was away on a sales trip in France when his child was born, and called him after his business venture, despite the fact that the boy's mother had already named him Giovanni, like Jesus' beloved disciple. Pietro Bernadone wanted the best for his son and ensured that the boy received the best possible education; that he always wore smart clothes and had smart friends. He was also pleased when Francis graduated as a young adult by going off to war, because he was destined for a gilded life full of accomplishments. As it happened, Assisi and Perugia were enemies at the time and Francis took part in what proved to be an unsuccessful battle. So he was imprisoned for a while. There he drove his fellow prisoners mad because he kept cracking jokes and was relentlessly cheerful.

Soon, though, he became ill, yet after his release he prepared to set off to war again, against another city-state, this time Apulia. He bought a fine suit of armour and started to prepare for the journey. As he got ready to leave for battle, he met another young soldier, a man who had fallen on hard times and whose clothing did not match his rank. So Francis gave him his own suit of armour and sent him on his way.

That night he had a strange dream. He was in a weapons store that was filled with suits of armour and cannons and guns. He asked whose they were and was astonished to be told that they all belonged to him. The following day he set off for the town of Spoleto, confident that he had everything he needed to be a successful soldier. Only another dream disturbed him that night too. This time he heard a voice asking him: 'Where are you going?' and he answered, 'To Apulia, to be a knight.' Then he heard the voice questioning him again: 'Who is it better to serve, the master or the servant?' 'The master,' he replied. The voice was insistent as it asked him a third question: 'Then why do you serve the servant instead of the master, the poor instead of the rich?' At that point he realized that God was speaking to him in his dream. So he asked: 'What do you want me to do?' And the answer was to lead to a series of dramatic choices that would change his life. 'Go home,' he heard the voice say, 'and you will be told what to do.'

So Francis gave up on soldiering and went back to Assisi. On his return his father gave a banquet for him at which Francis seemed moody and preoccupied. Pietro Bernadone assumed that the reason for this could be that his son had fallen in love. Even Francis' friends assumed the same. How else could they explain the change in the young man? When they asked him outright, he gave an astonishing answer. 'Yes, I have,' he replied, 'and she is nobler and richer and lovelier than any other.' He was talking about a vision he had glimpsed as a result of his experiences in prison and the dreams that followed. Rather than some fairytale damsel, his new bride was to be someone he called 'the Lady Poverty'.

If we remember Francis today and try to learn from his saintly life, it is because this vision became his loadstar. From now on, it would inspire all his choices, meaning that all the fine plans his father had made for him and which he had followed unquestioningly would unravel. He gradually came to see that coming closer to God meant not simply praying more and more intently; rather it was about his entire lifestyle and a whole new way of being. The main choices he had to make were ones that pained his father because they were all about turning his back on the rich bourgeois life for which his home and schooling had prepared him, and going instead for something totally different.

So young Francis had two things to grapple with and to try to understand. The first was about poverty and the second was about learning to be human in a new way. His was to be a journey of the spirit.

Learning by doing

Being of a practical turn of mind, Francis determined to go to Rome to visit the tomb of St Peter, the greatest of Jesus' apostles. From now on, he was determined that this would be the centre of his spiritual universe rather than the small town of Assisi where he was known as a rich boy and a rich man's son. When he got to Rome, he emptied his wallet, swapped clothes with a beggar and sat down on the ground at the tomb of St Peter, to beg for alms. He had arrived. Or so he thought. In fact his journey was only just beginning.

Fresh words eventually came to him from heaven. 'Francis, you must now learn to despise and hate what you have hitherto loved in the flesh, if you understand my will. And once you have begun to do this, you will find that all that was bitter and hard becomes sweet and pleasant, and that all you thought of with gloom and terror will bring you happiness and peace.' This offer was of conversion on a grand scale, and Francis was fearless in taking it up.

He returned to Assisi. On the road one day he met with a leper, was initially repelled by him but kissed his hand and gave him a gift. The leper pulled Francis towards him and kissed him on the lips. This simple act sealed the commitment he had made, to follow the Lady Poverty whatever might befall. Like St Paul on the road to Damascus, he now had his conversion moment. Soon afterwards he was to have further confirmation of his new call. He would often go to a tumbledown church near Assisi called San Damiano. While he was kneeling there praying one day, he heard Jesus calling him from the crucifix in the chapel where his naked suffering image was displayed. 'Francis, do you see that my house is falling down? Go and rebuild it.'

Francis took the charge literally. He gave money to the local priest so that an oil lamp could be bought to burn before the crucifix. Then he went home to try to raise funds to have the church rebuilt. When he got back to his father's house he spotted a bale of fine material, loaded it onto his horse and set off for the nearby town of Foligno. On the marketplace in front of the church of Santa Maria infra Portes he sold the material and the horse. He took the money straight back to San Damiano and gave it to the priest. Understandably he was nervous of accepting such a gift from this impetuous young man and refused it. Francis tossed the money onto a window ledge and took off for the woods. He found a cave and settled down to pray and live there.

Eventually, in 1206, he returned to Assisi, found his father and performed an action that profoundly shocked everyone. He stood in front of Pietro in public and took off all his clothes as a sign of a commitment to his new way of life. He only accepted the covering of an old tunic because the bishop, Guido of Assisi, who was called in to arbitrate, gave it to him. He marked a chalk cross on the back of it and set off for a new life in nearby Gubbio. Having been so literal in his understanding that he should rebuild the little church of San Damiano, he had much to learn about the interior life. Yet eventually his grand gestures would be matched by a real change of heart.

At Gubbio a tale was soon related about how he dealt with a wolf that had been stealing the local people's flocks and poultry. Francis fearlessly spoke to the wolf, saying: 'Brother Wolf, you have been making a lot of trouble round here. You have been mercilessly attacking God's creatures, and even God's image in human beings, and everyone is quite rightly complaining about you. But I want you to be at peace with the town, and I promise you that as long as you live the people of the town will feed you every day, but only provided you promise never again to do harm to man or beast.' He stretched out his hand and shook the wolf's paw on the agreement.

Later – only a year and a half before he died and when he was in great physical pain – he would write his great canticle of all creation, greeting all the elements of the known world and offering their praises to God.

> Most high, all-powerful, all good, Lord!
> All praise is yours, all glory, all honour
> And all blessing.
>
> To you alone, Most High, do they belong.
> No mortal lips are worthy
> To pronounce your name.
>
> All praise be yours, my Lord, through all that you have made,
> And first, my Lord, Brother Sun,
> Who brings the day; and light you give to us through him.
> How beautiful is he, how radiant in all his splendour!
> Of you, Most High, he bears the likeness.
>
> All praise be yours, my Lord, through Sisters Moon and Stars;
> In the heavens you have made them, bright
> And precious and fair.
>
> All praise be yours, my Lord, through Brothers Wind and Air,
> And fair and stormy, all the weather's moods,
> By which you cherish all that you have made.
>
> All praise be yours, my Lord, through Sister Water,
> So useful, lowly, precious, and pure.
>
> All praise be yours, my Lord, through Brother Fire,
> Through whom you brighten up the night.
>
> How beautiful he is, how gay! Full of power and strength.
> All praise be yours, my Lord, through Sister Earth, our mother,
> Who feeds us in her sovereignty and produces
> Various fruits and coloured flowers and herbs.
>
> All praise be yours, my Lord, through those who grant pardon
> For love of you; through those who endure
> Sickness and trial.
>
> Happy those who endure in peace,
> By you, Most High, they will be crowned.

All praise be yours, my Lord, through Sister Death,
From whose embrace no mortal can escape.
Woe to those who die in mortal sin:
Happy those she finds doing your will!
The second death can do no harm to them.

Praise and bless my Lord, and give him thanks,
And serve him with great humility.

This song is the earliest written piece of literature in the Italian language. Its simplicity makes it a literary and poetic masterpiece and it evokes the spirit of the Benedicite, a favoured prayer from the Anglican and Lutheran forms of Morning Prayer. The Benedicite comes from the Old Testament and is the song sung by Daniel's companions when they realized they had been saved from the fiery furnace prepared by King Nebuchadnezzar for their destruction. While it is a song of thanksgiving, Francis' outpouring reflects a knowledge of nature gained from hard experience, rather than anything sentimental. For while he was in Gubbio Francis too began to lead a wolf's existence, depending on the townspeople for his food and drink and working by day on his task of church rebuilding. He learnt about nature and the cycles of the sun and moon the hard way, by living exposed to the elements. He collected stones to take to San Damiano, he set about restoring St Peter's Church outside Gubbio and also Santa Maria Maggiore and Santa Maria dei Angeli, otherwise known as the Porziuncola. All in all this labouring took him three years.

Then, on the feast of St Matthias, 24 February 1209, Francis had another divine revelation. 'Take no gold, or silver, or copper in your belts, no bag for your journey, or two tunics, or sandals, or a staff.' The words come from Matthew 10.9–10. They go straight to the heart of the message of Jesus, and Francis heard them with extra-sensitive ears. Just as he had taken the charge to rebuild the church as being a literal command to restore San Damiano, so now he thought he should have nothing and live in complete dependency on God. Yet a strange thing happened, for at that precise moment he found he was no longer alone. Three companions came to join him: a merchant, Bernardo da Quintavalle; a cathedral canon, Pietro da Cattaneo; and another native of Assisi, one Edrigio, or Giles. What Francis found himself doing was founding a religious community of men who felt impelled to live in the same kind of radical way and who aspired to the same close relationship with God as he did.

Over the years their numbers would swell. By 1219 there were 5,000 brothers. Sisters too would join, making a separate community under the auspices of St Clare, and eventually a third order of lay people would follow a version of St Francis' way of life. Francis himself, meanwhile, was resolute in continuing on the path he had chosen under God's inspiration. He went on exploring what it meant to depend on God absolutely which, for him, involved complete poverty, doing without anything beyond essentials. He travelled too, broadening his horizons by visiting the Crusaders who were trying to win the Near East for Christian Europe. On a boat from Ancona to Cyprus he had 13 of his brothers with him, and they then travelled on to Acre and Egypt. He even visited the Sultan, Melek el Kamil, at Danietta before returning home via Jerusalem.

For this reason Francis is invoked as a patron of interfaith dialogue, where leaders and practitioners sit down and talk to each other about what their beliefs mean and how they can co-exist harmoniously in today's world. An irony is that the prayer so often invoked as a prayer for peace and seen as a mandate for this work cannot justifiably be attributed to Francis. He might have endorsed the sentiments but the words were first printed anonymously in French in 1912 on a holy picture which happened to bear his image. That is why it was assumed that Francis had written it and why it has been so widely quoted and adapted to be sung as a hymn.

Lord, make me an instrument of your peace;
Where there is hatred, let me sow love;
Where there is injury, pardon;
Where there is error, truth;
Where there is doubt, faith;
Where there is despair, hope;
Where there is darkness, light;
And where there is sadness, joy.

O Divine Master, grant that I may not so much seek to be consoled as to console;
To be understood, as to understand;
To be loved, as to love;
For it is in giving that we receive;
It is in pardoning that we are pardoned,
And it is in dying that we are born to eternal life.

One final episode from the life of Francis has to be narrated if we are to understand him properly. He never became a priest, choosing to remain a deacon. Yet God marked him out as a true follower of Christ when he received the stigmata in August 1224. This means that he received wounds on his hands and feet and in his sides, like the wounds of Jesus on the cross. One of his brethren, a friar named Leo, takes up the story:

> The most blessed Francis, two years before he died, spent Lent at Alverna in honour of the most blessed Virgin Mary, mother of God, and the most blessed archangel Michael. The hand of the Lord was on him throughout this time. He had the vision and conversation with the Seraphim as well as the impression of the wounds of Christ on his body.
>
> (*Little Flowers of St Francis*, Chapter 53)

From now on Francis' body was marked with the signs of Christ's sufferings just as surely as it had been by the rough tunic he had once worn in Assisi. The figure who had spoken to him from the painted image at San Damiano had come down from the cross and entered into the very fabric of his being. Francis too was destined to become an icon, a picture on which one could gaze to see something of the suffering of God. When he first undertook to follow the Lady Poverty, little did he know that he would be putting on Christ so literally. Yet that is what he did.

His ultimate home would be the goal of his final journey. Francis died as he had chosen to live, in utter simplicity. He insisted that he should be taken from his bed and lie naked on the ground to die. The date was 3 October 1226.

In 1210, Pope Innocent had ratified the existence of the Franciscan Order and Francis himself was canonized by the Church in August 1228. His feast day is celebrated on 4 October.

The message

So what was the secret of Francis' life and how is it applicable in today's world? To follow Francis, do you have to give up everything and literally have nothing? For him this was the formula that worked, and for some brave individuals it still will be. For the rest of us, the choice is not that simple, for we are tied into dense family networks where our fate and that of other people are too linked for us to act independently, with no care for our responsibilities towards others. What Francis teaches us is that there is a difference between the kind of poverty that is experienced as a social ill – and against which we should all fight – and poverty as an interior discipline or an attitude of mind.

The first kind of poverty leaps at us daily from our TV screens and newspapers when we see images of the world's poor and of their sufferings. It is a global phenomenon and needs global solutions. Yet global solutions sounds like rather a grandiose concept until we realize that as individuals we can support aid agencies and charities at both national and local level. Their work aims to ensure that the world's wealth is shared more equitably between us all. In this way we try to promote the idea that the riches of developed nations can work actively to help the poor. The key word is work or, in the modern slogan, trade not aid.

When he heard Jesus calling him to rebuild the church, Francis set about the task with his own hands. The rich merchant's son was not afraid of getting his hands dirty and of working with rubble and stones. His was a hands-on solution rather than a theoretical one. In this way he came to the greater realization that rebuilding the Church is about spiritual renewal and the change in attitudes that makes this possible. The same is true for rebuilding the world.

If we believe that God is a loving creator, then we have to believe that he has made enough to go round. Our task is to make sure that this redistribution happens. That is why Christianity – in common with many other of the world's faiths – has always advocated almsgiving, along with prayer and fasting. Yet Francis gave up his possessions for another reason altogether. He was not concerned with the world's poor or with the result of his actions on others. Rather he espoused poverty because he wanted to rely on God alone, instead of on the things he owned. Nowadays we are inclined to value both ourselves and others for our material possessions taken at face value. In a glittering world of celebrity and popular idols, Francis has a different message for us. True greatness, as he saw it, meant pursuing humility and a sense of selflessness, working for human transformation by imitating the humility and selflessness of Christ. He advocated a way of living that would transform us from the outside inwards. That is why he could never see prayer apart from action and why he offers us lifestyle choices.

The pattern of simplicity and order he espoused takes us to the heart of Christianity. For St Paul, in his Letter to the Philippians, had seen this before him,

> If then there is any encouragement in Christ, any consolation from love, any sharing in the Spirit, any compassion and sympathy, make my joy complete: be of the same mind, having the same love, being in full accord and of one mind. Do nothing

from selfish ambition or conceit, but in humility regard others as better than yourselves. Let each of you look not to your own interests, but to the interests of others. Let the same mind be in you that was in Christ Jesus,

who, though he was in the form of God,
did not regard equality with God
as something to be exploited,
but emptied himself,
taking the form of a slave,
being born in human likeness.
And being found in human form,
he humbled himself
and became obedient to the point of death –
even death on a cross.

Therefore God also highly exalted him
and gave him the name
that is above every name,
so that at the name of Jesus
every knee should bend,
in heaven and on earth and under the earth,
and every tongue should confess
  that Jesus Christ is Lord,
to the glory of God the Father.

(Philippians 2.1–11)

To choose poverty meant following the pattern Jesus set by choosing humanity, by being born as a human being and setting aside the divine glory. Because Francis was a literal kind of man he chose a way of life that would enable him to identify with Christ in this new way. For him, following the Lady Poverty meant having nothing that could protect him from his need for God. As he saw it, this kind of radical poverty was all about being human in a new way. As he saw it, his material needs were few and could be met by living quite differently from his parents, his family, even – eventually – his other followers.

Once again the series of choices he made has been widely misinterpreted, as though he simply advocated living close to nature. This is the reason he is invoked as a patron by the Green movement. The twelfth-century saint is seen as an early campaigner for simple sustainable living. We cannot know whether Francis himself would have been comfortable with that kind of label. For once again it rather misses the point. He did not embrace poverty in order to help other people. We are the ones who are asked to do that. He did not embrace nature in order to live closer to it. Again, we are the ones who are asked to do that. Rather he had his eyes fixed all the time on God and, as he understood it, God kept calling him to a more and more radical set of choices. The final one – to die naked on the ground – was his ultimate homecoming. The thin veil between him and heaven could finally slip away because he had no baggage, nothing to encumber him. God had become his all.

The legacy

So what is the true legacy for nowadays? I have suggested that we do Francis a disservice when we over-identify him with our own contemporary concerns, turning him into a patron for our own causes. By letting him be what he was, namely a great saint and a man of his times, with his own issues and concerns, we can discover a much deeper message.

Critically, Francis puts money in the frame. Many exemplary people trace a path to God that does not seem to involve anxiety about money or having a roof over one's head. Francis is not like this. All right, so he chose a radical solution to the problem, as he saw it, of being a nice, middle-class boy from a good home. He gave up everything. He cut through the temptations that surround us as people who are besieged with consumerist slogans and the call to spend more in order to live more. As the Lady Poverty became a reality for him, he deliberately chose a simple life, electing to do without anything superfluous in order to have her and have what she represented, namely union with God. In this way his prayer and the way he chose to follow Christ by living as he did came together. Not for him any of the barriers we are inclined to put up, as though God is only interested in the 'holy' bits of our lives and does not care about our financial concerns.

Francis teaches us that it is really important to bring everything to God and submit everything to the demands of the gospel. Anything else would be half-hearted. He trusted that he would still be able to enjoy the pleasure and joy of human living without the kinds of props most of us judge essential. At various times in his life he had to make a kind of audit, so he kissed a diseased leper and stripped naked in front of his father. He carried stones in his bare hands and braved the wolves. His body eventually was marked with the wounds of Christ and these were the battle scars he took to the grave.

Francis teaches us to find joy in deprivation, to live simply and not to make a big deal about this, to experience contentment. He encourages us to let go of anything that might make us less than fully human and to find our strength in God. As he wrote to his first brothers,

> Where love and wisdom reign, there is neither fear nor ignorance.
> Where patience and humility reign, there is neither anger nor disturbance.
> Where poverty and joy are found, there is neither love of money nor avarice.
> There is neither anxiety nor excess, where peace and meditation reign.
> Where the fear of God guards the heart, the enemy can find no way in.
> Where mercy and temperance live, there is neither too much nor too little of anything. (*Admonitions*, no. 27)

Love, wisdom, patience, humility, poverty, joy, peace, meditation, fear of God, mercy and temperance: all these qualities are offered to us by the lifestyle advocated by Francis of Assisi.

Francis teaches us to say thank you for what we have and not to crave for what we do not need. Above all, he teaches us contentment.

Some exercises to help you pray in the spirit of Francis of Assisi

1 Find the back of a large envelope and divide it into two columns. At the top of one write the words 'I have' and at the top of the other write 'I need'. Take your time to fill in the two columns with as much financial detail as you can. Be as honest as you can. Now add up the two columns and see if they tally or where the deficit lies. Finally, turn over the envelope and write out the two final lines of this chapter. See if you can say thank you and experience contentment.
2 Go back to the Canticle of the Sun, re-read it and choose your favourite verses from it. Write out the verse about water and pin it up in your kitchen by the taps. Say it often when you are at the sink. Write out your preferred verse and put it somewhere in your home or garden where it will surprise you and make you praise God spontaneously when you see it.
3 Go through your clothes and take anything you do not need down to a charity or thrift shop. Give it all away and notice what you feel.

All of these exercises are deliberately practical, because Francis was a practical man. They are intended to make you reflect about your lifestyle and to help you experience contentment. Say some extra prayers if you want to, but do not imagine that is a way off the hook of making some kind of practical audit of your values and aspirations. Be realistic.

3

Benedict, the father of community

A broken world

One of the most powerful images used to describe Christianity is that of the body of Christ. This is seen as a living entity where different parts have different functions yet all work together for the harmony and wellbeing of the whole because all are inspired by the same vision. From the earliest days Christians have tried to live together in model communities, reckoning that their way of life would be a witness to others of the greatness of God and that they would have a more direct experience of the life of Christ by holding their goods in common and sharing with each other.

The ideal is a simple one: the life of grace is not a personal possession, it is a gift, and gifts are for giving to other people, not for hoarding. So while Teresa and Francis, for instance, can offer us insights about prayer that will directly benefit us as individuals, this knowledge can also overflow and affect how we live as a human community. To understand how this can happen, we need to turn to the writings and ideas of another master of the spiritual life, St Benedict.

He was born in the city of Nursia in Italy in AD 480. The pagan Roman empire was a faded dream and well past its glory days. Some seventy years earlier, Alaric the Goth had invaded Italy, and when Benedict was born, Odoacer the Visigoth was in control. His days were numbered and another invader, Theodoric, king of the Ostrogoths, came to power when the boy was nine. In this fragmented world Christianity was something of a binding force, yet here too there was a snag, for Theodoric was an Arian Christian, which meant that his views on the Trinity were heretical, as he did not fully believe in the true divinity of Jesus Christ. He moved his capital away from Rome and built new palaces and churches in Ravenna, leaving the heart of the old empire as well as the papacy exposed.

Benedict was sent to study in Rome, and there encountered yet more conflict. For the pope, Gelasius I, died in 496 and his successor, Anastasius II in 498. The emperor Theodoric supported the candidacy of a deacon called Symmachus, who was duly elected – as was his rival, an archpriest named Laurentius, who was consecrated at St Mary Mayor's basilica. Theodoric took action. He had Laurentius banned and Symmachus installed as pope in his place. So the climate in which Benedict was raised was one in which the spirit of community was deeply fragmented, with both State and Church at sixes and sevens as rival groups fought over their different power bases. Everything seemed to be in tatters.

Benedict wanted things to be different. So his first experiments with the religious life were just that: experiments or ways of trying things out. He took off to Affile to the east of Rome and set himself up as a hermit. He chose to take a companion with him, his nursemaid, and one of the earliest legends about him concerns her. For she broke an earthenware sieve in half and Benedict found her weeping with distress. He held the two fragments together and they fused perfectly. However much or little truth there is to this story, it makes a nice metaphor, for Benedict's true vocation was to reconcile and heal and make broken things whole.

Leaving his nurse behind he then took off to the true wilderness, a place called Subiaco, 5 miles north of Affile and 40 miles from Rome. He found a cave and settled down to live on his own. A monk called Romanus befriended the young man and lent him books to read, so Benedict was able to spend his days in prayer and reading the Bible, Church Fathers and the lives of earlier Christian saints. The books were lowered to him in his cave on a rope, along with a ration of bread. For three years Benedict lived a life of perfect solitude, listening to the word of God as he was inspired in his prayers and reading.

Inevitably his reputation began to spread and other men wanting to lead a solitary life gathered around him. They lived in small groups and eventually there were 12 of these, each with 12 monks and its own abbot, and Benedict in overall charge. The mountainside at Subiaco was not big enough for them, and in 530 they set off to Monte Cassino in the Apennines. Here they found a former acropolis which had once been an encampment for Roman legionaries and showing evidence of a temple to Jupiter and a sacred grove. The monks used the stones they found there to build their new monastery and settled down to live together as a single community.

Later Benedict would write in his *Rule* for the monks that, 'It is to be desired that the monastery contain all that is necessary for life: water, a mill, a garden, a kneading trough, and that the various trades are exercised within the monastery walls, that the monks are dispensed from the necessity of going far away, which harms their souls' (chapter 66). What he sought for the group was self-sufficiency. The monks would want for nothing because he was not trying to devise an extreme way of life, consisting mainly of deprivation. Earlier monastic rules – particularly those coming from the eastern part of the Church – had envisaged something much more penitential, laying down regulations that would break the human spirit. Benedict wanted to create something more benign, a way of life that would enable people to realize their full human potential for the glory of God in a model community.

He uses a powerful image to set out his vision. The monastery would be a 'school for the service of God'. This makes the monks students or learners, constantly invited to grow and develop and do more for God. The *Rule* says it all,

> We are therefore now about to institute a school for the service of God in which we hope nothing harsh or burdensome will be ordained. But if we proceed in certain things with some little severity, sound reason so advising for the amendment of vices or the preserving of charity, do not for fear of this forthwith flee from the way of salvation, which is always narrow in the beginning. In living our life, however, and by the growth of faith, when the heart has been enlarged, the path of God's commandments is run with unspeakable loving sweetness; so that never leaving His school, but persevering in the monastery until death in His teaching, we share by our patience in the sufferings of Christ, and so merit to be partakers of His kingdom.
>
> (Prologue to the *Rule*)

What he envisaged was enlargement of the heart, a growth in openness to the grace of God, and to promote this he advocated stability, staying in the one monastery where everything would work harmoniously to help the monks find God. The school for the service of God would be a place where things that were harsh or burdensome were banned and sound reason would prevail to help the monks in their task.

One practice in particular marks out Benedict as an innovator. In older monasteries in the Near East, monks had to recite the Book of Psalms in its entirety, every single day. Benedict devised a routine whereby the psalms would be recited over a whole week rather than during a single day. In this way they could become a measured way of praying, rather than an assault course to prove spiritual athleticism. Seven times a day the brothers would gather in the monastic church or abbey and offer their prayers to God. Seven times a day they were offered the chance to immerse themselves in the word of God, so that it became a kind of river whose waters swept over them and entered their souls. This kind of schooling in prayer would bring the unspeakable sweetness he describes.

Community and communities

Benedict died in 547 and within 30 years his achievement lay in ruins, for in 577 Lombard soldiers came out of Hungary and destroyed Italy, laying waste to the monastery at Monte Cassino as they passed through. The monks were able to escape and they took with them their most treasured possession, the *Rule* that Benedict had written for them. We know about this because Benedict has a biographer, Pope Gregory, known as the Great. In 590 he became the first monk in the Church's history to be made pope, and his account of Benedict's life is a rosy one, replete with legends about the saint. Of the *Rule* he wrote,

> Amongst all the wonders which draw a shining halo around Benedict even in this world, we must count the splendour of his doctrine; for he has written a *Rule* for monks which is conspicuous by reason of its moderation and the clarity of its language. (Gregory I, *Dialogues II*, Chapter 36)

Moderation and clarity – two cardinal virtues for Benedict and for Gregory, and ones which, as they saw it, could help reorder the world. To learn about moderation in action and hear what it sounds like, we need to listen to the *Rule* itself. Now this turns out to be an aspiration Benedict would have approved of, for the *Rule* begins with that word: 'Listen', the aspirant monk is told.

> Listen, my son, to the precepts of your master, and incline the ear of your heart, and cheerfully receive and faithfully execute the admonitions of your loving Father, that by the toil of obedience you may return to Him from whom by the sloth of disobedience you have gone away.

Benedict had learnt how to listen with the 'ear of his heart' while living in the solitude of his retreat at Subiaco. Now he lays out guidelines for a way of life where a whole group of people can learn inner attentiveness and hear God speaking in their hearts. This is his chief legacy; this is what makes his *Rule* a holy text. So who is the monk to listen to? God, evidently, but also the abbot or father of the monastery, as well as the other monks. 'Disobedience' comes from a Latin word that means not hearing; that is why it can only be countered by listening. A monk can learn obedience, true listening, by living an attentive way of life.

So the whole way of monastic life is geared to this objective: obedience or listening. Monks make vows. They promise God that they will practise stability, namely that they will stay in one place as members of one community; they promise obedience, committing themselves to listen to God in this one place; and they promise 'conversion of manners', namely an inner conversion to the way of life practised in this one place. Their vows affect everything they think and are and do. By promising to be located in a specific place they avoid being flighty or running away from temptation. The voice of God becomes part and parcel of the very fabric of everything around them, including their fellow monks.

People of the Rule

Chief among these is the father abbot, who has a very particular vocation, for his job is to make sure that everything in the monastery is ordered to the good of all. In the *Rule*, Benedict sets out the context within which he wants the abbot to operate and defines the checks and balances that will ensure that his job is always to serve and not to lord it over the monks in his care.

> An abbot to be fit to rule a monastery should ever remember what he is called, and in his acts illustrate his high calling. For in a monastery he is considered to take the place of Christ, since he is called by his name as the apostle saith, 'Ye shall receive the spirit of adoption of sons, whereby we cry Abba, Father.' Therefore the abbot should neither teach, ordain, nor require

anything against the command of our Lord (God forbid!), but in the minds of his disciples let his orders and teaching be mingled with the leaven of divine justice.

The abbot should ever be mindful that at the dread judgment of God there will be inquiry both as to his teaching and as to the obedience of his disciples. Let the abbot know that any lack of goodness will be accounted the shepherd's fault. On the other hand, he shall be acquitted in so far as he shall have shown all the watchfulness of a shepherd over a restless and disobedient flock: and if as their pastor he shall have employed every care to cure their corrupt manners, he shall be declared guiltless in the Lord's judgment.

The abbot in his teaching should always observe that apostolic rule which saith, 'reprove, entreat, rebuke' (2 Tim. 4:2). That is to say, as occasions require he ought to mingle encouragement with reproofs. Let him manifest the sternness of a master and the loving affection of a father. He must reprove the undisciplined and restless severely, but he should exhort such as are obedient, quiet and patient, for their better profit.

The abbot ought ever to bear in mind what he is and what he is called; he ought to know that to whom more is entrusted, from him more is exacted. Let him recognise how difficult and how hard a task he has undertaken, to rule souls and to make himself a servant to the humours of many. One, forsooth, must be led by gentle words, another by sharp reprehension, another by persuasion; and thus shall he so shape and adapt himself to the character and intelligence of each, that he not only suffer no loss in the flock entrusted to his care, but may even rejoice in its good growth. Above all things let him not slight nor make little of the souls committed to his care, heeding more fleeting, worldly and frivolous things; but let him remember always that he has undertaken the government of souls, of which he shall also have to give an account. (Chapter 2)

The abbot takes the place of Christ, so he has a servant role and should model himself on the good shepherd Jesus describes in the Gospels. Yet his care for the many means he should never forget the few; both the ninety-nine and the one wandering sheep require his attention. He should adapt his instructions 'to the character and intelligence of each', which means knowing every monk in his care as an individual and respecting this individuality. The charge is an immense one, a great calling, and nowadays there are many outside of the obvious setting of the monastery who turn to Benedict and his *Rule* for advice on how to organize themselves as corporate managers, or even as fathers of families. They recognize that there is something uniquely humane in Benedict's guiding principles that brings out the very best in other people by allowing them to grow through sound schooling.

Benedict developed another key concept which has much to teach those who are in positions of authority in today's world, for it goes against the wisdom of today's corporate living.

> Whenever any weighty matters have to be transacted in the monastery let the abbot call together all the community and himself propose the matter for discussion. After hearing the advice of the brethren let him consider it in his own mind, and then do what he shall judge most expedient. We submit to what he shall deem best. As it becometh disciples to obey their master, so doth it behove the master to dispose of all things with forethought and justice.
>
> In all things, therefore, everyone shall follow the *Rule* as their master, and let no one rashly depart from it. In the monastery no one is to be led by the desires of his own heart, neither shall any one within or without the monastery presume to argue wantonly with the abbot. If he presume to do so let him be subjected to punishment according to the *Rule*.
>
> The abbot himself, however, must himself do all things in the fear of God and according to the *Rule*, knowing that he shall undoubtedly have to give an account of his whole government to God, the most just judge.
>
> If anything of less moment has to be done in the monastery, let the abbot take the advice of the seniors only, as it is written, 'Do all things with counsel, and thou shalt not afterwards repent of it.' (Chapter 3)

The insight is a simple one: wisdom lies not only with the 'seniors' in any grouping; younger people too can bring insights to the deliberations of the community. Indeed, the older members are to meet on their own only to discuss matters of 'less moment' that will have less impact on the whole group. There is a saying that the most recent person to enter a stuffy room is the one who can identify that the windows need to be opened. This, in a nutshell, is what Benedict was saying.

Is this the reason why he took the principle of subsidiarity so seriously, namely the idea that we should delegate tasks to the person who is most fitted to undertake them? My favourite example is that of the cellarer, the monk whose job it is to ensure that the monks get enough to eat and drink. Benedict describes the kind of man who should be chosen for this task, and then ensures that he should be equipped and trusted to get on with the job.

> Let one of the community be chosen as cellarer of the monastery, who is wise, mature in character, temperate, not a great eater, not arrogant nor quarrelsome, nor insolent, and not a dawdler, nor wasteful, but one who fears God and is as a Father to the community. Let him have the charge of everything; do nothing without the abbot's order; see to what is commanded, and not make the brethren sad. If any of them shall perchance ask something unreasonable he must not vex him by contemptuously rejecting his request, but humbly and reasonably refuse what he wrongly asks.
>
> Let him look after his own soul, mindful of the Apostolic principle, that 'they that ministered well, shall purchase to themselves a good degree' (1 Tim. 3:13). Let him take every care of the sick, of children, of guests, and of the poor, knowing that he shall have to render an account of all these on the judgment day.
>
> Let him look upon all the vessels and goods of the monastery as if they were the consecrated chalices of the altar. He must not think anything can be neglected; he must not be covetous, nor a prodigal wasting the goods of the monastery;

> but let him do everything with forethought and according to the direction of his abbot.
>
> And above all things let him have humility and give a gentle answer to those to whom he can give nothing else, for it is written, 'A good word is above the best gift' (Ecclus. 18:17). Let him take charge of all the abbot shall commit to him, but let him not meddle with anything which is forbidden him. Let him provide the brethren with their appointed allowance of food without impatience or delay, so that they be not driven to offend, being mindful of the divine word which declares the punishment he deserves, 'Who shall scandalise one of these little ones. It were better for him that a millstone should be hanged about his neck, and that he should be drowned in the depth of the sea' (Matt. 18:6). If the community be large let him be given helpers, by whose aid he may without worry perform the office committed to him. What is given let it be given, and what is asked for let it be asked at suitable times, so that no one be troubled or distressed in the House of God. (Chapter 31)

Everything in this chapter of the *Rule* tends to the absolute requirement that 'no one should be troubled or distressed'. Benedict has the realism to acknowledge the central importance of food and drink, especially in a community where many are involved in hard physical work, tending the fields and crops, taking care of vines and olives and generally putting their backs into all that has to be done. So he is adamant: everyone should have enough to eat; indeed, their food should be regarded as an allowance, a natural right. The *Rule* is also realistic about how much the monks should receive to drink:

> 'Everyone hath his proper gift from God, one thus, another thus' (I Cor. 7:7). For this reason the amount of other people's food cannot be determined without some misgiving. Still, having regard to the weak state of the sick, we think that a pint of wine a day is sufficient for any one. But let those to whom God gives the gift of abstinence know that they shall receive their proper reward. If either local circumstances, the amount of

> labour, or the heat of summer require more, it can be allowed at the will of the prior, care being taken in all things that gluttony creep not in.
>
> Although we read that 'wine is not the drink of monks at all,' yet, since in our days they cannot be persuaded of this, let them at least agree not to drink to satiety, but sparingly, 'because wine maketh even the wise to fall away' (Ecclus. 19:2).
>
> (Chapter 40)

At every turn Benedict is shown to be caring and humane. He values wisdom and maturity and ensures that nothing should infantilize the brethren. He is anxious to provide a way of life that both supports and is sustained by prayer. The *Rule* is divided into 73 chapters, of which three deal with poverty (33, 34 and 54) and one with work (48). His interest is less in generalizations, heady formulae of pious aspirations, and more in attention to what will make the life of the community work and work well for the good of all. So he lays out rules about clothes and beds and books and pens and, as we have seen, food and drink. Everything is ordered to help everyone in every particular.

The work of God

At the heart of the *Rule* lies the understanding that there is work to be done, the opus Dei, the work of God. So what is this great work and how can those of us who are attracted by the spirit of Benedict's *Rule* and his humanity share in it? The *Rule* is insistent: the work of God is the Divine Office, the prayer of the monks, the heartbeat of their common life. From the moment they rise in the morning at dawn and celebrate Lauds, the first of their Offices together, until the moment they file away from the abbey church at night having completed Vespers together, they are invited to serve God by the work of prayer. Lauds, Prime, Tierce, Sext, None, Vespers and Compline punctuate the day and are sustained by other slow, meditative readings of the Scripture and private contemplation, when the monks pray alone in the silence of their own hearts.

This daily pattern is sustained by a vision of the whole liturgical year. For Benedict the greatest feast day in the Christian calendar is Easter Sunday. So Lent, as a time of preparation for Easter, is to be kept as an especially solemn season. Summer time runs from Easter to 1 November, and then winter time begins. Weekly rhythms too ensure that the march of time is carefully observed, Sunday being its natural pinnacle. This was the day when the cooks and the readers in the monastic refectory were to change over their rotas.

The legacy

The *Rule* of St Benedict is practical, benign and deeply scriptural. It gathers its energy from the prayerful recitation of the words of the psalms and from an attentive listening to the Scriptures. Benedict's own use of the Bible is interesting, the fruit of his own obedience to the word of God. So he writes, 'The Scriptures rouse us when they say: "It is high time for us to arise from sleep" (Rom. 13:11)' and goes on to add, 'What page, what passage of the inspired books of the Old and New Testaments is not the truest of guides for human life?' He listens attentively and hears the Bible say that these words are 'medicine' and 'a light that comes from God', rather than a series of proof texts laying out mandatory rules that have a global application. He does not use the Bible to score points, but rather goes to its inner wisdom and applies this judiciously.

If you visit a Benedictine monastery – and I do regularly, as I attend Mass at Downside Abbey in Somerset – certain things will strike you. I love the anonymity presented by the sight of monks as they file out to celebrate together, their black habits matched by their cowls. While a monastery necessarily produces grand characters, it also values humility in the brethren, and as they process into the abbey choir, each becomes less than himself because each is swept up into a greater mystery. Then there is the sound, a great tolling bell that can be heard across the countryside and that calls everyone to prayer, whoever they are and wherever they are working, and also the music as the monks' voices fill the nave with their chanting. Gregorian chant, the soundtrack to the opus Dei, inexorably floods out to the congregation as they begin the liturgy of the day.

Benedict died in 547. He insisted that he should be taken to the chapel of St John at Monte Cassino, and stood there praying until he had no more strength and died. His biographer, St Gregory the Great, wrote:

> Six days before he left this world, he gave order to have his tomb opened, and forthwith falling into an ague, he began with burning heat to wax faint, and when as the sickness daily increased, on the sixth day he commanded his monks to carry him into the oratory, where he armed himself with receiving the body and blood of our Savior Christ; and having his weak body held up by the hands of his disciples, he stood with his own arms lifted to heaven. As he was praying in that manner, he gave up the ghost. On that same day two monks, one being in his cell, and the other far distant, had one and the same vision concerning him: they saw all the way from the holy man's cell, towards the east even up to heaven, hung and adorned with tapestry and shining with an infinite number of lamps. At the top a man, reverently attired, stood and demanded if they knew who passed that way, to whom they answered saying, that they knew not. Then he spoke to them: 'This is the way by which the beloved servant of God, Benedict, ascended up to heaven.'
>
> By this means, as his monks that were present knew of the death of the holy man, so likewise those who were absent, by the token which he foretold them, had intelligence of the same thing. He was buried in the oratory of St John Baptist which he himself had built when he overthrew the altar of Apollo. That cave in which he first dwelled [at Subiaco], even to this very time, works miracles, if the faith of those that pray there requires the same. (Gregory I, *Dialogues II*, Chapter 37)

Without the *Rule*, this is all Benedict would be, the object of pious legend. Because of the *Rule*, his wisdom and humanity live on, freshly interpreted and incarnated for us by the monks who follow it to this day. Benedict was canonized by the Church in 1220 and his feast day is celebrated on 11 July.

Some exercises to help you pray in the spirit of Benedict of Nursia

1 Get hold of a copy of the *Rule* of St Benedict. You can find the whole text online at sites such as <http://www.ccel.org/ccel/benedict/rule2/files/rule2.html>. Read it carefully and decide which bits are applicable to you in your daily circumstances.
2 Write out a list of the various communities you belong to: for instance, family, neighbourhood, workplace, city or town. Think about ways in which you could help make each of these more tolerant and benign. List the particular virtues you could try to practise in each of them, such as listening to the opinions of others, giving people more space and time, allowing their ideas to flourish. Put these virtues into practice. There are seven days in the week; try to concentrate on the needs of each group on a different day so that you are committed to practical outcomes.
3 Take out a map and try to locate the Benedictine community closest to your home. In the UK this may be a ruin because of the effects of the Dissolution of the Monasteries during the reign of Henry VIII, or it could be a living community. Either way visit the monastery and try to cast yourself into the mindset of the people who first lived and worked there for the glory and praise of God. You will be surprised to discover how many monasteries are right on your doorstep once you start looking. Make monastery-spotting a regular

feature of your holiday programme, particularly if you go driving in Europe. Try to attend a service in a monastery and consider buying a CD so that you can take the sound away with you and play it in your car or home.

4

Ignatius of Loyola and knowing what to do next

Seeking and finding God's will

Benedict described how a whole community should live under obedience to the will of God. Ignatius of Loyola, a great sixteenth-century innovator, showed how individuals could discover God's personal will for them. He adds another unique dimension to the praying repertoire of the Christian Church.

Born in 1491, at the castle of Loyola in the kingdom of Navarre, now the Basque province of Guipúzcoa, Íñigo was the youngest of 13 children. When he was 7 years old his mother died. When he was 15 the young boy became a page in the service of a relative, Juan Velázquez de Cuéllar, who was treasurer of the kingdom of Castile. As a *hildalgo* or nobleman he was destined for army service and enlisted in 1517. Four years later he saw decisive action. The Spanish forces with whom he was serving were defending the small town of Pamplona against the French. Because they were outnumbered, his companions wanted to surrender, but Ignatius persuaded them to fight on. But then a cannonball took him out of the fray and he was returned to the family home at Loyola on a bier, his leg shattered and his splendid dreams of heroism in tatters.

In his *Autobiography* he takes up the story, describing how his leg had to be reset when he arrived home and how he then insisted on a further operation once it became clear that he would be disfigured. Without surgery he would have had one leg shorter than the other and a protuberance growing out of it. This would not do because, as he described, he 'had made up his mind to seek his fortune in the world'. While convalescing from the butchery, he found he could not stand and demanded that books should be brought to him in his bed. He had been used to reading what he calls 'worldly books of fiction and knight errancy', but all the castle at Loyola could supply were religious books. These included a life of Christ and lives of St Francis and St Dominic. So he set to and read them avidly.

Then he began to notice something interesting. These books inspired him in a positive way. Previously, when he had read romances, he had also felt inspired and used to fantasize about what he would do in the service of the fine ladies he read about. He could pass days imagining the feats he would accomplish. But then the dreams would fade and he would be left feeling dissatisfied. With the stories of Francis and Dominic, something quite different happened. The inspiration lasted. So he writes that he would

> pause and reason with himself. 'Suppose that I should do what St Francis did, what St Dominic did' . . . When he was thinking of the things of the world he was filled with delight, but when afterwards he dismissed them from weariness, he was dry and dissatisfied. And when he thought of going barefoot to Jerusalem and of eating nothing but herbs and performing other rigours he saw that the saints had performed, he was consoled, not only when he entertained these thoughts, but even after dismissing them he remained cheerful and satisfied.
>
> (*Autobiography*, Chapter 1, 8)

Ignatius' autobiography, dictated years later in 1553 to one of his Jesuit brethren, namely Father Luis Gonzales, is in the third person. He dwells at length on those months of transition at Loyola, perhaps because he realized that they were crucially formative in everything he was to become. For what Ignatius was learning on his sickbed was the power and value of discernment, namely sifting through his own experience to discover where God's will lay for him. When he felt distracted and ultimately bored by the courtly romances, he saw that they were leading him away from God, and when he felt liberated by the heroism of the saints, he believed that he was being drawn towards God. He described these two sets of feelings as desolation and consolation, and learning about them became part of his own inner fine-tuning, for they would help him learn the will of God for him in every particular.

He tells us that 'part of his time he spent in writing, part in prayer'. Then came moments of distillation, as this worldly young soldier began to lay aside the defences of his previous way of life and to face the reality of his conversion. He took to going out at night, to look at the sky.

> It was his greatest consolation to gaze upon the heavens and the stars, which he often did, and for long stretches at a time, because when doing so he felt within himself a powerful urge to be serving our Lord. He gave much time to thinking about his resolve, desiring to be entirely well so that he could begin his journey. (*Autobiography*, Chapter 1, 11)

The journey was to be a long one and it would take him to Montserrat in the Basque mountains, to a small town called Manresa some three miles away, to Barcelona, Venice, Jerusalem, Paris and eventually Rome. The interior journey too was to be as extensive, taking him through extremes of penance, poverty, service, years of study, the companionship of the early Jesuits who gathered around him and his development of a wonderful tool for the spiritual life, namely his Spiritual Exercises. What both these journeys had in common was their shared objective: God's will.

His first steps on the road again come in the form of a story. He had determined to go to the shrine of Our Lady of Montserrat, the home of the statue of a black Virgin holding the Christ child. This was a twelfth-century statue much venerated in Catalonia. On the way he met a Moor riding on a mule and fell into conversation with him. All began amiably enough, but then they got to discussing Mary's virginity, which the Moor found impossible to accept. How could she have remained a virgin after giving birth, the man wondered. Ignatius was incensed, thinking that the honour of the Blessed Virgin Mary was under threat. Then the Moor trotted off, leaving Ignatius' blood boiling. 'A desire arose to go in search of the Moor and give him a taste of his dagger for what he had said.'

What happened next? Ignatius decided to let his mule make the decision. Either it would follow the Moor who had taken a road that veered off the main highway to a village, or it would go straight on. He dropped the reins and waited. Recalling the event, he said, 'It was the Lord's will that, although the village was only thirty or forty steps away, and the road to it broad and even, the mule took the royal highway and passed by the village road.' So the Moor's life was spared and Ignatius headed on his way to Montserrat. In future he would learn that there are more adequate ways of discovering God's will than something so arbitrary as dropping the reins of your donkey.

Arriving at the monastery, he confessed all the sins of his past life to one of the monks. Then he sought out a beggar, swapped clothes with him as a sign of the new identity he was putting on and went to the great abbey church. Here he prayed all through the night, alternately kneeling and standing, his fine sword and dagger hanging at the altar of Our Lady, a pilgrim's staff in his hand. The following day he set out for Manresa, the place of his next transformation.

If you type the words 'Manresa' and 'Ignatius' into an Internet search engine you are likely to get some 27,700 hits, for the words have become synonymous with 'finding your true vocation', and so Jesuit noviciates, where young men undergo training to become followers of Ignatius worldwide, are inclined to be called Manresa. But over the past ten years or so the concept of Manresa has been extended to mean any enterprise that can help individuals find what God is calling them to. So, for instance, at Marquette University's website we learn,

> The Manresa Project assists the Marquette community in exploring what it means to serve God. For some, that service will take the specific form of religious life, priesthood, ordained ministry or lay ministry in the church. Others will serve God as parents or single people in a variety of professions.
>
> As Christians, whatever life paths we take will be marked in special ways if we bring our values and faith into our decision-making. Think of it this way: If you are a manager, are you a different kind of manager because of your Christian beliefs? If you are a teacher or nurse or doctor or lawyer, does your Christian perspective inform and shape what you do and how you treat others?
>
> We think so, and the Manresa Project offers several programs to help you begin defining that difference.

What follows is a list of important questions. The Internet searcher is exhorted to:

> Think of the Manresa Project as a starting point for identifying your potential. You are beginning a journey and each day you travel, every encounter with another person, every decision you make – big or small – form the road you're on.
>
> A good way to begin finding your way is by asking yourself these questions:
>
> Who am I?
>
> How do I want to live my life?
>
> What gifts and talents do I have?
>
> What are the needs of the world and how can I use my gifts and talents to meet them?
>
> How do faith and belief in God intersect with my life, my choices, my plans, my decisions, my behaviour?

> Your answers will lead you through something called discernment. This is a process of the heart through which you define your personal response to God's call. You sense your vocation.
> <http://www.marquette.edu/manresa/about/index.shtml>

'You sense your vocation.' That is what Ignatius did at his Manresa and that is the experience offered to all those who follow after him, whether as members of his Society of Jesus or as lay followers of his spirituality.

For at Manresa, Ignatius too asked himself those kinds of questions. He also went to extremes in his quest to understand God's will, for he adopted a penitential lifestyle and began to have strange visions. In his *Autobiography* he says,

> Every day he begged alms in Manresa. He ate no meat, drank no wine, although both were offered him. On Sundays he did not fast, and he drank the little wine that was given him. Because he had been quite delicate about caring for his hair, which in those days was quite the vogue – and he had a good head of hair – he made up his mind to neglect it and to let it grow wild, without combing or cutting it or covering it either day or night. For the same reason he allowed the nails of his hands and feet to grow, because here too he had been excessive. While he was in this hospital, it often happened to him in broad daylight to see something in the air close to him, which gave him great consolation because it was very beautiful. He could not make out clearly what the thing was, but somehow it appeared to have the form of a serpent. It was bright with objects that shone like eyes, although they were not eyes. He found great delight and consolation in looking at this thing, and the more he saw it the greater grew his consolation. When it disappeared it left him displeased. (*Autobiography*, Chapter 3, 19)

Anyone who starves gets hallucinations, and Ignatius was no exception. What made him different was what he did with his strange experiences, for he worked through them and came out the other side, cut his hair and his fingernails, determining to go to Jerusalem as a pilgrim. He associated the bad visions with the feelings of desolation he had had at the castle of Loyola when his spirits had dipped during his convalescence. Equally he connected the consolation of true prayer with the feelings he had experienced when reading the lives of St Francis and St Dominic. The ten months he now spent living and praying at Manresa beside the river Cardoner would bear fruits for the rest of his life and lead him eventually to schematize all he had discovered and to write down his Spiritual Exercises.

The Spiritual Exercises

The rest of his story can be told quite simply. He did get to Jerusalem. He then realized that he needed to gain some sort of education and so headed for the Sorbonne in Paris before attracting companions and gathering them together to live in community as the first members of his Society of Jesus. It flourished immediately, gaining some heroic early members such as St Francis Xavier, missionary of the Indies. At the time of his death in 1556 Ignatius was living in Rome, writing letters to Jesuits in all parts of the known world and holding together a huge body of talent as more and more young men swelled the ranks of his Society of Jesus. Ignatius was beatified on 27 July 1609 and canonized by Pope Gregory XV on 12 March 1622, along with St Francis Xavier. Ignatius' feast day is celebrated by the Jesuits and by the universal Church on 31 July, the anniversary of the day he died.

Just as Benedict left both a religious community and a written text, his *Rule*, as his legacy to the world, so too Ignatius gave both a community of men dedicated to the service of the 'greater glory of God' and also a living text that encapsulates everything he learnt about how human beings can come close to God. The book of the Spiritual Exercises (as opposed to the Exercises inside the book) is essentially a manual. It is meant to be used by someone who is guiding a person making the Exercises through a process. So it begins with a few recommendations about what kind of a person that should be.

A nice image best catches the attitude of this 'retreat director'. He, or frequently nowadays she, is to be like a 'balance at rest', swayed neither towards one outcome nor to another. In this way, they 'should permit the Creator to deal directly with the creature, and the creature directly with his Creator and Lord'. Ignatius wanted the individual making his Exercises to experience the same clarity he had felt when he gazed up at the stars of his nights at the castle of Loyola, and that meant having a direct experience of God without anyone getting in the way.

So who would this individual be? Basically, anyone facing a big life choice. What they would go through would be a process whereby, through prayer and reflection, they would arrive at a point where the options would be clear to them and they could both make the choice and then have time to see it confirmed by God. Ignatius himself dealt with men who were thinking of becoming followers of the Jesuit way of life and also other professional people who had to be getting on with their own daily lives, so he built a level of flexibility into the programme he prepared. Indeed, he says that, 'The Spiritual Exercises must be adapted to the condition of the one who is to engage in them, that is, to his age, education, and talent.'

So there are some people who are free to take time out of their daily lives to make a long retreat, lasting 30 days in a special retreat house where everything is provided for their needs – from silence to food to daily visits from the retreat director, or 'the one giving the exercises', as Ignatius prefers to call him/her. In this place five hours are set aside for prayer daily and the one making the exercises goes through an experience similar to that Ignatius lived through at Manresa, though without the excesses he submitted himself to. Alternatively, the programme can be adapted for those who want to make the Exercises in daily life, giving up an hour and a half to prayer each day and seeing their director once a week or so.

Whichever mode is chosen, the practice is the same. There are four 'weeks' of Exercises to be gone through, each of which has a different purpose and outcome. During the first week, the one making the Exercises prepares for the encounter with God that makes knowledge of his will possible. That means stripping off all pretences, acknowledging oneself as one truly is. So there are opportunities to think about the grace and mercy of God and, of course, one's own sins, just as Ignatius did when he first arrived at Montserrat. Then, during the second week, we follow the life of Christ, from the moment of the incarnation and through his public ministry. Ignatius is keen to see how attractive that life is to us, just as he himself was drawn to the lives of the saints at Loyola. Does the person making the retreat want to serve under the banner of Christ? To get involved in the ministry of the Church in spreading the gospel and all its values? To work for change and to make the world a better place for others?

And if they do, are they ready for a big choice, an election to follow Jesus into the third week, namely as he prepares for his passion, suffering on the cross and death? Only then can they follow him towards the resurrection, to the transformation where everything can be freely received as a direct grace from God, the giver of every good. The aims of the Exercises are the liberation of the human spirit to seek and find God in all things and growing friendship or intimacy between the soul and God.

Ignatian contemplation

So much for the big picture. But there are other exercises too, namely techniques that Ignatius teaches within the *Spiritual Exercises* as a way of helping us to pray. One of the most popular of these is a method of contemplation which frees up the imagination to come to the service of the praying individual. As an example, I am going to look at his contemplation on the nativity from the beginning of the second week of the *Spiritual Exercises.* Remember, the retreatants will have been praying for a clear knowledge of themselves and of God's all-forgiving grace. Now they are getting ready to hear a call to service. In this particular exercise there is a preparatory prayer where 'I will beg God our Lord for grace that all my intentions, actions and operations may be directed purely to the praise and service of His Divine Majesty' (Exx. 46).

This instruction has two presuppositions. First, the responsibility for setting time aside for prayer lies solely with me. I have to give myself generously, with the grace of God, so that all I hope for, all I want and all I do is bound up with this activity. Second, I am in the presence of the 'Divine Majesty', for his praise and service. Like Ignatius the knight in his vigil of prayer at Montserrat, I am preparing for service in the presence of my Lord and King.

Ignatius lays out the game plan: he next provides me with three 'preludes', that is to say, three ways of preparing my 'intentions, actions and operations' for what is to follow:

> First prelude. This is the history of the mystery. Here it will be that our Lady, about nine months with child, and, as may be piously believed, seated on an ass, set out from Nazareth. She was accompanied by Joseph and a maid, who was leading an ox. They are going to Bethlehem to pay the tribute that Caesar imposed on those lands.

This instruction is directed to the memory. I am to remember the facts, as given in Luke's Gospel, but with a little twist, for nowhere in the Gospel do we read that a maid accompanied Mary as she and Joseph made their way to Bethlehem. This detail is an add-on, an invention of a sixteenth-century Spanish nobleman who cannot imagine otherwise. And this is the point.

By using his imagination, Ignatius is able to enter more deeply into the story – and now he invites us to do the same thing.

> Second prelude. This is a mental representation of the place. It will consist here in seeing in imagination the way from Nazareth to Bethlehem. Consider its length, its breadth; whether level, or through valleys and over hills. Observe also the place or cave where Christ is born; whether big or little; whether high or low; and how it is arranged.

Very few of us have been to Bethlehem, and the city we see nowadays is very different from the place described by the Gospel. So what are we to do? Let our imaginations take over. We are to 'see in imagination'. Like a theatre director, I am invited by Ignatius to set the scene, to let my mind flood with pictures and to explore them. If I really let go I may find myself in a totally unexpected landscape, so I need to take a good look at it. Another twist: if I look closely at the path, I will discover how hard or easy it is to negotiate, both for the holy family – and for me. Despite my protestations I may discover that I put up obstacles in my heart to the grace of God and here I can see the shape of them and how they are configured. That is why I need Ignatius' next prelude as it inspires me to search my heart.

> Third prelude. This is to ask for what I desire. Here it will be to ask for an intimate knowledge of our Lord, who is become man for me, that I may love Him more and follow Him more closely.

So with the scene set and with hearts ignited, I now move into the scene.

> First point. This will consist in seeing the persons, namely, our Lady, St Joseph, the maid, and Child Jesus after His birth. I will make myself a poor little unworthy slave, and as though present, look upon them, contemplate them, and serve them in their needs with all possible homage and reverence. Then I will reflect on myself that I may reap some fruit.

Taking on the guise of 'a poor little unworthy slave' I too 'look, contemplate and serve'. By looking, by seeing what is going on, I can contemplate, become still in the presence of what I see and then find out what I can do to help. Contemplation for Ignatius becomes 'contemplation in action', a desire to put my hand to the plough. That is why I am to 'reflect on myself', that is to say, make some practical application of the truths revealed to me by my imagination.

After looking, I have to do the same thing all over again. Only this time I have to listen. Our full repertoire of senses is called into play.

> Second point. This is to consider, observe, contemplate what the persons are saying, and then to reflect on myself and draw some fruit from it.

The pattern here is to 'consider, observe and contemplate' and then to 'draw fruit' by listening to the response that is evoked in our imagination. Finally, in the third point, notice what everyone in the scene is doing and what they have done to make the birth of Jesus possible. I am to notice the pattern. The Saviour who is born for me is the Saviour who will die for me.

> Third point. This will be to see and consider what they are doing, for example, making the journey and labouring that our Lord might be born in extreme poverty, and that after many labours, after hunger, thirst, heat, and cold, after insults and outrages, He might die on the cross, and all this for me. Then I will reflect and draw some spiritual fruit from what I have seen.

The final act is to put into words everything I have seen and experienced during this time of prayer.

> Colloquy. The exercise should be closed with a colloquy. I will think over what I ought to say to the Three Divine Persons, or to the eternal Word incarnate, or to His Mother, our Lady. According to the light that I have received, I will beg for grace

to follow and imitate more closely our Lord, who has just become man for me.

Close with an Our Father.

(Exx. 111–116; *The Spiritual Exercises of St Ignatius*, trans. Louis J. Puhl, SJ, Loyola University Press, Chicago, 1951)

This prayer is Trinitarian, that is to say, it is directed to each person in the Blessed Trinity or to Jesus himself or to his mother. I am to 'beg for grace' to ask God for the energy and hope and expectation that I will 'follow and imitate' the Lord more closely, 'according to the light that I have received'. Ignatius offers balance and harmony, for I have to be realistic about what I can do and to appraise my own desires. The Lord's Prayer brings the session to a close with its set formula of words grounding me back into the traditional rhythms of Christian prayer.

The assumption that Ignatius makes is that the imagination is my friend. It has secrets for me which will tell me more about myself and my relationship with God than a simple repetition of the words of the text, even read slowly and meditatively. By using his technique, my soul is revealed to God and God to my soul in a new way. With such immediate access to the language of pictures and symbols, we lose the controls that we normally exercise and enter into a new place in prayer and a new relationship with God.

This technique has been taken up and used in all sorts of different ways to help people know themselves and their deep desires. Fantasy exercises abound; they are used in retreat houses, spirituality centres and also in schools of management or in corporate business training. For instance, I could pretend I am going on a journey. In my imagination I get into a train and look around it carefully. I look at the carriage and see if it is full or empty; if I am alone or accompanied; what the weather is like outside the windows. Only then do I look at the luggage label on my suitcase and realize where I am going.

All sorts of hopes are locked in our subconscious or unconscious, and exercises such as these can unlock them for us, so they are often used in self-awareness groups or for counselling. What makes Ignatius remarkable is that he discovered the insight long before famous psychiatrists such as Freud or Jung revealed how important the unknown world of our deep desires can be in directing our lives. And he did so in a context of prayer and discernment, helping us to discover God's will for us as individuals.

The direction of his *Spiritual Exercises* is all-important, for its goal is not about self-improvement or being more effective in the workplace. The motto of the Society of Jesus is 'All for the Greater Glory of God'. This was the guiding principle of Ignatius' own life; by entering into the mindset of the Spiritual Exercises and practising personal discernment, it can become ours as well.

Some exercises to help you pray in the spirit of Ignatius of Loyola

1 Identify someone you really admire and read a book about them. At the end write down the principles that motivated them and the qualities they exemplified. Resolve to put those principles and qualities into practice in your own life. Then re-read Mark's Gospel and notice the qualities Jesus displays in his life as Mark tells it. Again write them down as you go along and resolve to do like him. Resolve to imitate Christ.

2 In his *Spiritual Exercises* Ignatius gives us this prayer: 'Take, Lord, and receive all my liberty, my memory, my understanding, and my entire will, all that I have and possess. Thou hast given all to me. To Thee, O Lord, I return it. All is Thine, dispose of it wholly according to Thy will. Give me Thy love and Thy grace, for this is sufficient for me' (Exx. 234). Say it slowly, a phrase at a time, and repeat it often.

3 If you face a big personal decision, this can be a very helpful exercise. Phrase a question with a 'yes' or 'no' answer to it. For instance, 'Should I look for a job now and save further studies for later?' or 'Should I move house to be nearer work/my girlfriend/the zoo or whatever?'

Then choose a place some 20 minutes away from your home and go for a walk towards it, imagining that the answer is 'yes' and that you are moving closer to your goal. On the return journey, as you walk back home again, imagine that the answer is 'no' and that you are turning down that particular choice.

As you walk be careful to notice things that would ordinarily pass you by, such as how warm or cold it is, if there is a wind and where it is coming from; if the light is shining in your eyes or on to the path in front of you; if there is rubbish or trash on the ground; if there are flowers or weeds, evidence of growth or of decay. Look up at the billboards and see what they have to say to you; sniff the air and see what things smell of. Open your senses to experience everything on your path. Censor nothing; notice everything. Pray to know God's will for you as you walk, and really pump up the sense of 'yes' or of 'no'. By the end of the walk, even if you are absolutely clear about the outcome, write down everything you noticed and see where God's will is calling you through what attracts you and what fails to attract you. Pray in thanksgiving for any light you have received – and remember the exercise to use it another time.

5

The Jesus Prayer

Prayer from the east

Any consideration of Christian prayer would be incomplete without looking at some of the riches that come from other parts of the tradition, for instance the Jesus Prayer, which is from the eastern or Orthodox part of the Church. The story of the first great split of the Church into west and east is long and complicated, with politics and geography and ambition and power struggles all having their part to play. A visit to the holy places in a city such as Jerusalem is living evidence of this far-off conflict and demonstrates how deep its roots – and consequences – go. Rival Churches play out roles that were designated by conflicts long ago in the past. The site of the Holy Sepulchre itself is a case in point, as Christians continue to fight over who did what, where and when and how the basilica should be managed. For years the keys to the building were kept by a Muslim, to ensure equality of access to all the warring parties.

Yet from the Orthodox Church comes one of the most mysterious and benign forms of Christian praying: the Jesus Prayer. This grouping of Christians is made up of the Greek Orthodox, Antiochian Orthodox, Russian Orthodox, Orthodox Church and the Byzantine Church, all comprising a single entity, nowadays usually called the Eastern Orthodox Church. Their orthodoxy comes from the fact that they are all ancient and that they adhere to the teachings of the first seven great councils of the whole Church, as do the Churches of the west.

Division only came in 1054, when the east and west Churches became irreconcilably divided – the Great Schism.

The Jesus Prayer dates to before the Great Schism, so it constitutes a legacy of a happier time when Byzantium could talk to Rome and share the treasures of its spirituality without conflict and division. For the prayer's origins, we need to look at a text from St Paul's First Letter to the Thessalonians, 5.17, where we read that the people of Thessalonia are to 'pray unceasingly' as they await the return of Jesus in his second coming. So the context is clear; yet this recommendation does not come on its own: it is part of a package of virtuous acts which will ensure that we are ready for the coming of the Lord, whenever that is. Paul writes,

> And we urge you, beloved, to admonish the idlers, encourage the faint-hearted, help the weak, be patient with all of them. See that none of you repays evil for evil, but always seek to do good to one another and to all. Rejoice always, pray without ceasing, give thanks in all circumstances; for this is the will of God in Christ Jesus for you. Do not quench the Spirit. Do not despise the words of prophets, but test everything; hold fast to what is good; abstain from every form of evil.
>
> (1 Thessalonians 5.14–22)

The charge on us to pray at all times comes along with two other recommendations: to rejoice and to give thanks. They are about attitudes of the heart. That is why the Jesus Prayer is sometimes called the Prayer of the Heart. The prayer is simple to recite, as all you do is repeat over and over again the words, 'Lord Jesus Christ, Son of God, have mercy on me a sinner.' The idea is to inhale on the first six words, taking in the presence of Christ on your breath, and to exhale on the rest, letting go of your sinful self. In this way the prayer becomes rhythmical and can grow to be as natural as the act of breathing itself. Some practitioners in the east use a little rope or cord with knots in it, and pass these through their hands as they say the prayer, counting their beads as they go. In the understanding of the Eastern Church, as recorded in the writings of an early desert father, St Hesychois the Priest, from the collection of sayings known as the *Philokalia*, 'The more rain falls on the earth, the softer it makes it; similarly, Christ's holy name gladdens the earth of our heart the more we call upon it.' The image is doubly powerful because it comes from the desert, where the appearance of rain is in any case something of a luxury. This attitude of openness to God has been expressed in the western tradition by hymns such as Charles Wesley's,

> O thou who camest from above
> The fire celestial to impart,
> Kindle a flame of sacred love
> On the mean altar of my heart.
>
> There let it for thy glory burn
> With inextinguishable blaze,
> And trembling to its source return
> In humble prayer and fervent praise.
>
> Jesus, confirm my heart's desire
> To work and speak and think for thee;
> Still let me guard the holy fire
> And still stir up the gift in me.
>
> Still let me prove thy perfect will,
> My acts of faith and love repeat;
> Till death thy endless mercies seal,
> And make the sacrifice complete.

Where St Hesychois used an image of water falling on the ground to soften it – again, a singularly pleasing sight in the desert – Wesley uses the vocabulary of sacrifice and the image of fire. He insists that the Christian heart should be a place of meeting, where God's gifts are received and our desires are transformed. We are to 'work and speak and think for thee'; that is to say, be centred and focused on the life of faith within. By being Christ-centred we become Christ-like. In Wesley's final verse he advocates repeating acts of faith and love, and the Jesus Prayer is just one such means to focus and centre the human heart and all our emotions.

The shape of the Jesus Prayer

The prayer begins by naming Jesus and with a profession of faith, namely the earliest of the creeds, which stated simply that 'Jesus is Lord'. For its inspiration and for that of the Jesus Prayer itself, we need to turn to the story related in Luke 18, where a blind man turns to Jesus for help.

> As he approached Jericho, a blind man was sitting by the roadside begging. When he heard a crowd going by, he asked what was happening. They told him, 'Jesus of Nazareth is passing by.' Then he shouted, 'Jesus, Son of David, have mercy on me!' Those who were in front sternly ordered him to be quiet; but he shouted even more loudly, 'Son of David, have mercy on me!' Jesus stood still and ordered the man to be brought to him; and when he came near, he asked him, 'What do you want me to do for you?' He said, 'Lord, let me see again.' Jesus said to him, 'Receive your sight; your faith has saved you.' Immediately he regained his sight and followed him, glorifying God; and all the people, when they saw it, praised God. (Luke 18.35–43)

Luke neatly inserts this story into the final chapter of his account of the public life of Jesus, who is now on his way to suffering and death in Jerusalem. Indeed, in the preceding verses he has just given his apostles a warning of what is to happen:

> Then he took the twelve aside and said to them, 'See we are going up to Jerusalem, and everything that is written about the Son of Man by the prophets will be accomplished. For he will be handed over to the Gentiles; and he will be mocked and insulted and spat upon. After they have flogged him, they will kill him, and on the third day he will rise again.' But they under-

> stood nothing about all these things; in fact, what he said was hidden from them, and they did not grasp what was said.
> (Luke 18.31–34)

The apostles' lack of comprehension is highlighted by the contrast with this little story of the blind man. For we are told that he received his sight, followed Jesus and gave glory to God, thereby becoming a true believer and disciple in his turn. The words 'Lord Jesus, Son of God, have mercy on me a sinner' commit us to do likewise.

Practising the Jesus Prayer

We usually say 'practice makes perfect', but in the case of the Jesus Prayer, practice probably makes for more practice. There is no getting to the end of it. You do not do it to be able to tick a box and say, 'Well, that's done'; it is, quite literally, more a way of life. Most practitioners would agree that there are two different ways of using it, one formal, the other informal. The formal practice of the prayer means saying it over and over again for a period of some ten to fifteen minutes every morning or evening. The idea is to find a quiet place, to sit with a straight back and to begin. To hold your attention you might like to use a lighted candle or an icon to gaze at. As the prayer takes you over, notice two things. First, that any rhythmic and self-conscious breathing exercise such as this has an automatic effect: it slows you down. Allow yourself to enjoy this experience by saying the words more slowly, and notice how you feel.

This practice of slow repeated prayer is not unique to Christianity. Indeed, there are some who say it is an import from the east, for many Indian religions ask for similar disciplines. The use of a mantra dates back to earliest times, when gurus would encourage their followers to pray by repeating the word 'aum', meaning the whole of reality, created and uncreated. Mantras were first written down in Sanskrit and their practice spread through Hinduism, to Buddhism and Sikhism. British television has even carried a successful comedy series where the practice is parodied. In *Absolutely Fabulous* the character called Edina Monsoon (played by Jennifer Saunders) falls back on the technique whenever she is stressed out, which is often.

Neither the association with non-Christian religions nor the ease with which the practice of repetition can be made fun of deterred the desert fathers and mothers who first took it over. The point, for them, is that it worked. By repeating a formula with words taken from Scripture, they found themselves entering more deeply upon the Christian way. The prayer stills the heart along with the breath and makes people who practise it more reflective and focused, as with any breathing exercise. But there is a second insight attached to the practice of the Jesus Prayer, as anyone who uses it soon realizes.

The sense of smell is the oldest of our senses because it is closely associated with food and so with survival. When we breathe in, we exercise this function. Most of our senses share a common feature with the rest of our bodies, namely one side of our brain operates them. That is why people who have had a stroke in their left brain lose the power to move in the right-hand side of their bodies, and vice versa. The left hemisphere controls our ability to use language and do mathematics, abstraction and reasoning; the right hemisphere looks after our visual and spatial skills. And keeping the two together, so that they talk to each other and co-ordinate us, is the corpus callosum, which is placed between the two. Whichever way you look at it, the brain is an amazingly complicated organ. Yet the sense of smell is one of its most refined and simple functions because it is not routed or bifurcated like this.

The left nostril feeds directly into the base of the left side of the brain and the right nostril into the right. As you breathe slowly you will notice that you have a predominant or lead nostril and that it changes about every 20 minutes, naturally allowing the other one to take over. During the day, try holding your hand above your upper lip and breathing out through your nostrils. You will notice immediately which nostril is leading and also that it changes at regular intervals.

What has all this to do with prayer? Well, it prepares you for one consequence of practising the Jesus Prayer, namely that your sense of smell is your friend. Let it become a trigger for you, to inspire you to use the prayer at other times, as the occasion takes you. This is the second, or informal, use advocated by the desert monks. They thought it important to send constant 'arrows of prayer', as they called them, winging their way between us and God. The Jesus Prayer requires no book, no special place. You can do it anywhere, and that is what the desert tradition recommends.

It is this sheer adaptability of the Jesus Prayer that makes it especially useful in times of personal or national disaster. I can be worrying about all the problems of the world and yet still be praying as I walk down the street or sit at my computer, because the Jesus Prayer is like a swelling sea, rising and falling in my heart, forming a backdrop to my thinking and anxiety about the bigger picture or my private worries. It goes on in the background and gradually emerges into the foreground, becoming an indestructible bedrock to my conscious thoughts.

In another version of the story of the blind man, we read in Matthew's Gospel that,

> As Jesus went on from there, two blind men followed him, crying loudly, 'Have mercy on us, Son of David!' When he entered the house, the blind men came to him; and Jesus said to them, 'Do you believe that I am able to do this?' They said to him, 'Yes, Lord.' Then he touched their eyes and said, 'According to your faith let it be done to you.' And their eyes were opened. Then Jesus sternly ordered them, 'See that no one knows of this.' But they went away and spread the news about him throughout that district. (Matthew 9.27–31)

Jesus has just healed the daughter of Jairus, so the blind men certainly had news to spread – and this is the charge they take up. The difference in this account is that there are two blind men, and Matthew highlights the fact that they name Jesus as 'Son of David'. There are some versions of the Jesus Prayer that also use this title.

It serves to emphasize Jesus' humanity, as well as being the title that Matthew uses in the genealogy he gives at the start of his Gospel. This genealogy traces the human roots of Jesus through stories familiar to students of the Hebrew Scriptures, introducing him as the 'son of David, son of Abraham' and finally, after listing his lineage, naming 'Jacob the father of Joseph . . . of whom Jesus was born, who is called Christ' (Matthew 1.16, RSV). He wants to call attention to Jesus' Jewishness, to prove he is the Messiah and saviour of his people. Pray with Matthew's title, 'Lord Jesus, son of David, have mercy on me, a sinner' and you get a different slant on the prayer. Nothing is written in tablets of stone. Or try another form, 'Lord Jesus, son of the living God, have mercy on me, a sinner.' All of these are permitted and all have scriptural roots.

Luke has a parable story in his Gospel which supplies a further variant, this time with the words 'God be merciful to me, a sinner' forming the main focus. Jesus teaches about true prayer as an attitude of the heart when he says,

> Two men went up to the temple to pray, one a Pharisee and the other a tax-collector. The Pharisee, standing by himself, was praying thus, 'God, I thank you that I am not like other people: thieves, rogues, adulterers, or even like this tax-collector. I fast twice a week; I give a tenth of all my income.' But the tax-collector, standing far off, would not even look up to heaven, but was beating his breast and saying, 'God, be merciful to me, a sinner!' I tell you, this man went down to his home justified rather than the other; for all who exalt themselves will be humbled, but all who humble themselves will be exalted.
>
> (Luke 18.10–14)

This focus concentrates on inner attitudes. An observer, looking at the scene from the outside, would take for granted the moral superiority of the Pharisee. After all, he is a true believer and everything he does with his life proves this, so to an onlooker he looks squeaky-clean. The tax-collector or publican, as someone who has dealings with the Roman occupying force and collects money for them, can be written off without further consideration. He is clearly a moral reprobate and a personal wreck. Yet the Pharisee revealed proud thoughts that held God at bay, while the publican spoke to God from the heart of his need. That is why his prayer was heard and he was justified.

'A sinner' in the presence of God

The tax-collector was justified – and so too are we. That is the message of the Jesus Prayer. That is why it is a healthy prayer. This is worth underlining because there are those who would claim that it is psychologically unhealthy to name oneself as a sinner. They reckon the modern cult of the healthy ego cannot handle such robust language. In their eyes, the desire and need to be seen as successful and as high achievers overrules all other considerations. To admit that we are less than perfect is seen as weak. It labels us as failures. That is why people find it so hard not simply to admit to others that they have done wrong, but even to face up to the fact themselves. Clearly, this is not the work of a healthy ego, but of one in denial, and in this sense the wisdom of the Christian tradition runs contrary to the so-called wisdom of our age. A healthy ego is one which is realistic, and by naming ourselves as sinners we are doing no more than facing up to the truth.

The Jesus Prayer is not asking us to revel in this insight, or to roll around in the mud of the human condition. Rather it insists that the encounter with our Saviour should be a genuine one. To name myself as a sinner is to acknowledge my need of God. That is why Charles Wesley asked God to kindle fire on the 'mean altar' of his heart. The Jesus Prayer is prayer addressed to the heart and prayer that betrays the true attitude of our heart; prayer addressed to our personality and prayer that betrays our personality.

It seeks maturity and that is why it cannot really help people whose psyche is not robust enough to handle it. The novelist J. D. Salinger, famous for *The Catcher in the Rye*, has compellingly described the consequences of praying with the Jesus Prayer when we are not strong enough to deal with its realism. In his novel *Franny and Zooey*, two stories about the Glass family and set in 1955, we learn that Franny, who is attending a liberal arts college in the USA, has taken up with a book called *The Path of the Pilgrim*. The novel describes a disastrous weekend that she spends with her boyfriend, Lane Coutell, for a football match at his college. Their initial meeting at the railway station goes well enough. Then comes a meal at a restaurant during which Franny goes white in the face and feels faint with effort as she has to listen to the young man's pretentious boasting about his English Literature course and a recent A-grade for an essay. The more he brags and boasts, the more she retires into her shell, barely eating a chicken sandwich or drinking her glass of milk while he swaggers his way through snails, frogs' legs and salad.

She begins to recite the Jesus Prayer, all the while smoking cigarette after cigarette. When she stands up to make a second escape to the ladies' room she passes right out, collapsing in a heap on the floor. Her weekend has ended disastrously, as has her young man's. In the second story, we see nothing further of Lane. Instead, Franny is lying on the sofa in her parents' New York apartment, with the cat, Bloomberg. Her actor brother, Zooey, emerges from a bath, during which his anxious mother, Bessie, disturbed him. The source of her anxiety: Franny. Zooey is commissioned to sort out his sister. What follows in fictionalized form is a fascinating commentary on the Jesus Prayer.

For the Glasses are no ordinary family. As children all seven of the offspring had starred in a US radio show called *It's a Wise*

Child, in which they had been able to show off their prodigious memories and intellectual talents. The history of religion and philosophy came as naturally to them as that of literature and music. Indeed, Franny had found her little green book *The Path of the Pilgrim* lying on the desk of her older and now dead brother, Seymour. Zooey's attempts to get through to her take us on a tour-de-force trip through the history of Russian mysticism. Zooey makes his sister examine her own motivation for trying to use the Jesus Prayer. His point is that, as he says,

> There is something about the way you're going at this prayer that gives me the willies, if you want to know the truth. You think I'm out to stop you from saying it. I don't know whether I am or not – that's a goddam debatable point – but I *would* like you to clear up for me just what the hell your motives are for saying it. As a matter of simple logic, there's no difference at all, that *I* can see, between the man who's greedy for material treasure – or even intellectual treasure – and the man who's greedy for spiritual treasure.

When he finally succeeds in making his point, he pins down the fatal flaw in Franny's practice.

> I'd like to be convinced that you're not using it as a substitute for doing whatever the hell your duty is in life, or just your daily duty. Worse than that, though, I can't see – I swear to God I can't – how you can pray to a Jesus you don't even understand.

Zooey has identified two fatal misunderstandings in her use of the prayer: she is seeking to avoid her 'daily duty' and, a nice Jewish girl, is praying to someone who is a mixture of all her best fantasies. He lists these, starting with her lost brother,

> If you're going to say the Jesus Prayer, at least say it to Jesus, and not to St Francis and Seymour and Heidi's grandfather all wrapped up in one. Keep him in mind if you say it, and him only, and him as he was and not as you'd like him to have been.

Wise words from the 25-year-old actor. For Zooey is making a serious pitch for reality and truth in Franny's use of the prayer.

Only then can it hope to serve her on her spiritual path. The alternative? It becomes a block and a hindrance in her life, preventing her from doing what a twenty-year-old girl should do, such as going out with her boyfriend and enjoying the cup of chicken soup her poor benighted mother keeps trying to offer her.

He says,

> Even if you went out and searched the whole world for a master – some guru, some holy man – to tell you how to say your Jesus Prayer properly, what good would it do to you? How in hell are you going to recognize a legitimate holy man when you see one if you don't even know a cup of consecrated chicken soup when it's right in front of your nose?

So where does wisdom lie? The message of Franny and Zooey is apparently simple, for Seymour had handed it over to Zooey when the young man was a child and just starting out on *It's a Wise Child*. The boy was convinced that the producer was a moron – and the studio audience and the announcer too. Yet Seymour told him to shine his shoes before leaving home. Given that this was radio and given that no one could see their feet where the children sat round their table in the studio, Zooey was outraged. So Seymour added,

> 'Shine them for the Fat Lady', and Zooey did, that night and on all subsequent nights. Truth lay in respect and fidelity. He concludes, 'This terribly clear, clear picture of the Fat Lady formed in my mind. I had her sitting on this porch all day, swatting flies, with her radio going full-blast from morning till night. I figured the heat was terrible, and she probably had cancer – and I don't know. Anyway, it seemed goddam clear why Seymour wanted me to shine my shoes when I went on air. It made *sense*.'

And so to the final revelation:

> I'll tell you a terrible secret. *There isn't anyone out there who isn't Seymour's Fat Lady*. Don't you know that? Don't you know that goddam secret yet? And don't you know – listen to me now –

> don't you know who the Fat Lady really is? . . . Ah, buddy. Ah, buddy. It's Christ himself. Christ himself, buddy.
>
> (J. D. Salinger, *Franny and Zooey*, Penguin Books, Harmondsworth, 1955)

So finally, abandoning her misuse of the prayer, Franny gets into bed, smiles quietly at the ceiling and falls into a deep dreamless sleep.

Seymour's insight about the importance of even the smallest of our everyday duties and respect for other people and the true 'fruit' of the Jesus Prayer are one and the same thing. St Paul had encapsulated this when he wrote to the Corinthians about Jesus' obedience to the Father, 'When all things are subjected to him, then the Son himself will also be subjected to the one who put all things in subjection under him, so that God may be all in all' (1 Corinthians 15.28). Everything comes together and has meaning when it is subjected to God in Christ. The Jesus Prayer is no more than a tool, and one to be used carefully, as an act of intercession, not as some piece of mumbo-jumbo. Its purpose is to bring us to the moment of total resolution, when God does become all in all.

'Be merciful to me'

Is this why the Jesus Prayer has us pray for mercy? Tied up with our personal identity as sinners is the understanding that the gift we most need from God is mercy. This is a profoundly scriptural word that appears 239 times in the Bible. In the Old Testament God comes to dwell on his mercy seat, namely the solid gold covering that was placed on the Ark of the Covenant in the Temple in Jerusalem. To beg for mercy is to ask to approach God, to come into the divine presence and to remain there. 'Be merciful to me, a sinner' we pray, knowing full well that we should expect the full blaze of the anger of God, of divine justice for our sinfulness, yet confident that what we in fact find is forgiveness, divine mercy in action.

That is why the psalms make the point that God's mercy is to be repeated in our own behaviour. We too are to show mercy in our turn. Psalm 112 is uncompromising: 'Happy are those who fear the LORD, who greatly delight in his commandments . . . They rise in the darkness as a light for the upright; they are gracious, merciful, and righteous' (vv. 1, 4). In the New Testament we find Jesus' take on this: in Luke's Gospel, just after he has spoken the words of the Beatitudes, commending the poor, the hungry and those who weep, Jesus says: 'Be merciful, just as your Father is merciful.' In this lies true perfection.

The Jesus Prayer will have worked for us if it leads us to come before God as sinners and to receive the divine mercy from the hands of our Saviour; it will have worked if, in our turn, we show mercy to others and fulfil the 'daily duties' of everyday life, knowing that Christ is our 'all in all'. No wonder it takes some practising, for this sort of resolution and completeness is a life's work.

Some ways to use the Jesus Prayer creatively

1 Get to church five minutes early on a Sunday and sit using the Jesus Prayer as you prepare for the service to begin. Notice what happens to you as your breathing slows and you become responsive to the word of God.

2 Get hold of a copy of the anonymous Russian classic, *The Way of a Pilgrim* or the sequel, *The Pilgrim Continues his Way* and read the full collection of stories that describe the pilgrim's search for wisdom in nineteenth-century Russia. Alternatively, read J. D. Salinger's *Franny and Zooey* and make up your own mind about the story.

3 Try using the Jesus Prayer last thing at night and see if you can fall asleep over it. Ask God to keep the 'mean altar' of your heart as a place of prayer overnight so that you may wake up to acts of faith and love the following day.

6

On pilgrimage to Taizé

The road to Taizé

Over the past 60 years, Burgundy in France has become home to a place that is synonymous with the Christian life. In earlier times, as a medieval traveller you might have headed to Burgundy for the cuisine or the wine, or to visit the great monastery at Cluny where, from the year 910, a Benedictine community of monks established what became known as the largest monastery in the west. It was a massive centre of scholarship and learning and a place of pilgrimage on a grand scale.

Nowadays though, Cluny lies in ruins and you are more likely to take the TGV from Paris to go to Macon and then the local bus to Taizé, the home of a community of Brothers who practise an intensive ministry of hospitality. Expect to see plenty of young people among your fellow travellers, for the whole orientation of the place is towards them. Expect to see an international array of visitors, for the entire spirit of the endeavour speaks of openness to the whole world. As the bus trundles through prosperous farmland and neat little villages with exotic place names that read like the wine pages of some newspaper supplement; as it makes its steady way across south-facing slopes scored with vineyards and large, furry cattle grazing on the other fields, you are transported in space and in time too. You are going towards a parable, a way of living community that has a powerful message for us all. You are safe to take all your own anxieties and problems and uncertainties with you because you will be able to speak of them there and will find that the burden lightens. At the heart of this community lies prayer, and this is the lure that draws you.

Taizé is at once a place, and a place of pilgrimage, for people come here from every nation under heaven to find God. And it is also an inspiration, something you can take home with you and make live in your own context. There are no T-shirts or baseball hats with logos for you to buy and wear as a groupie; you cannot 'join' as this is not a movement; all you can do is kneel where, in T. S. Eliot's words, 'prayer has been valid', and let God do the rest. This double focus of invitation to be there and profit from the experience, but also to go home and get on with the rest of your life is neatly summed up in the mission statement given on the Taizé website at <www.taize.fr/en>.

> From its beginning the community has been inspired by two aims: to live in communion with God through prayer and to be a leaven of peace and trust in the midst of the human family.
>
> A stay at Taizé is an opportunity to seek communion with God in prayer, singing, silence and reflection. It can be possible to rediscover an inner peace, a meaning to life and a new impetus.
>
> Experiencing a simple life shared with others, they realize that daily life, as it stands, is the place where Christ is waiting for them.
>
> Some young people are looking for ways of following Christ for their whole lifetime.
>
> A stay in Taizé can help discern this call.

Taizé: a place, an experience, a style, a sound and a community

Taizé's own vocation is to help people search for meaning. Each evening, after the night prayer, the Brothers stand and listen to the unburdening that goes on when a line of young or not-so-young pilgrims forms and people speak from the heart. It is a place where you can ask deep questions about how to make sense of your life and find comfort. That is why so many of us go there on pilgrimage. As well as being a place, it offers an experience, a style, a sound and a community.

The experience is easy to describe because it is all about meeting God and meeting other people. When you get there you take part in an 'accueil', a greeting or welcome where you will be told where you are to pitch your tent or find your sleeping quarters, shown where to find your food and given directions for the church. Most people arrive on a Sunday afternoon and stay for a week so as to let the spirit of the place take a hold on them and to benefit from the Bible studies which are an integral part of the stay. That first day you will part with some money, enough euros to pay for your board and lodging or maybe a few extra to help subsidize the stay of someone less well off than you are.

The shape of each day people spend with the community is very simple: it begins and ends with prayer. Morning prayer at 8.15 is followed by breakfast and then workshops where groups gather and are led in Bible reflection by one of the Brothers. More prayer at 12.15 leads on to lunch, a free afternoon, though with some chores thrown in for good measure. People are inclined to linger over a cup of tea, coffee or hot chocolate at the end of the afternoon, before attending another workshop or watching a video of the history of the place, and then they enjoy supper before the night prayer that rounds off the day. There is no sense of coercion, but rather an eager willingness to go with the very simple flow, punctuated as it is by prayer and meals. These can be taken in silence, but a principal part of the attraction of Taizé is meeting up with other people, other searchers, and so a shared meal becomes a welcome rendezvous with friends. That is all part of the experience. It is also where visitors meet up with something very distinctive about the style of Taizé, namely its simplicity.

Meals are dished up on brown plastic trays. The food is served by whoever happens to be at the head of the queue when it arrives at the service area. Mountains of mashed potatoes go straight onto your blue plastic plate, along with, say, a hard-boiled egg, a piece of cheese, apple and yoghurt. Your soup is served into the same red plastic bowl that at breakfast held tea or coffee and, because this is France, there is always bread. Or it might be that you have a dollop of chilli con carne with lashings of rice, followed by an orange and a pot of Petit Filou. Either way the plates and bowls are the same and the washing up is done by hand by another group of volunteers. The food is filling and comforting, but no one would go to Taizé for its *gastronomie*; that would be to miss the point. The food and the way it is served are part of an experience of simplicity which is the place's hallmark. To eat it you are given a large spoon and soon become adept at learning to stir tea with one end and spread jam with the other.

When I first went there some 20 years ago, I formed a mixed impression of the experience, largely because it was a really hot summer and the water had to be turned off each afternoon. This meant that the lavatories smelt terrible. These days they retain their simplicity but are clean, and the blocks that house them are well cared for. If you like, they are just about the most substantial buildings on the site because they are made of stone rather than wood. Most of the other barracks are temporary wooden structures, so meetings and workshops have a feeling of impermanence that is very much part of the Taizé style. You take what you can from them because you are not here to stay for a long time, but to make your way back to your own life and your own Christian community.

The community you find at Taizé does its most intense living in the church, for that is where the Brothers and their visitors meet to pray. The first thing that strikes you as you go in through large wooden flaps is that this is like a large tent. One wall is covered in swathes of dark orange material, lamps burn in little candle stands. As your eyes become accustomed to the light, you realize that the lamps are in fact clustered around icons. These show the figure of Christ on the cross, an image of the resurrection, of Mary the mother of Jesus, of Jesus himself in the company of someone identified simply as 'a friend'.

The Brothers gather together for prayer, kneeling on simple wooden prayer stools as the church fills with rows of silent young people. And then the music begins, the sound of simple chanting, the sound that encapsulates the meaning of Taizé. For the prayer sessions are central to what Taizé is all about. There is light and dark, music and silence, word and gesture, a minimum of commentary and no exposition. What is on offer is cut down, streamlined, simple, as 'pure' as the white of the Brothers' prayer robes, which contrast strikingly with the amber wall of the church, the golden glow of myriad lights.

The prayer is offered to God, obviously, but it is also offered to all the visitors as an example, a way of coming into the presence of God and stripping down to essentials; for what Taizé provides is a setting for inner awareness. The chants are simple protestations of faith and trust, their words repeated over and over, rather like the Jesus Prayer. Typically they have a natural flow: 'Lord, Jesus Christ, your light shines on us. Let not my doubts or my darkness speak to me. Lord Jesus Christ, your light shines within us. Let my heart always welcome your love' (© Taizé). The effect of this, especially sung on a dark December night, is memorable. And so too with the prayers of intercession which recall a needy world. Unlike many such invocations, they do not turn into mere shopping lists of the world's ills or of human greed and culpability. Rather they speak of the change of heart that will affect human behaviour and so transform society: 'God of all love, if our hearts sometimes let us down, you call us quite simply to abandon ourselves to you' (© Taizé). This is a place where self-offering becomes possible, even desirable.

Taizé is also a community. The Brothers are marked out at times of prayer by the white robes they wear. Otherwise they wear clothes that suit the work they do, taking care of the premises and grounds, making the distinctive ceramics from the sale of which they earn their livelihood, or preparing for the yearly gatherings they hold both at home or in the capital cities of Europe. Sometimes as many as 5,000 people a week can pour through the place during the summer, from some 75 different countries. Equally, the yearly European meetings can draw crowds of tens of thousands, all of them bent on replicating a Taizé experience but also on bringing it home to the place where they live. The two meetings held in London in the 1980s certainly made that clear to me. I went along to sing and also to meet up with young people from across the continent, confident that we had something important to share, as was the case. At the beginning of 2008, the European meeting was held in Geneva. Beforehand the community received goodwill messages from the Pope, the Archbishop of Canterbury and Orthodox Patriarchs of both Moscow and Constantinople, as well as European political leaders and the Secretary General of the United Nations. The contribution the Brothers make to community building is recognized on a grand scale.

They were especially delighted by the insight of Rowan Williams, the Archbishop of Canterbury, when he wrote saying,

> Dear Brother Alois and friends of the Taizé Community, dear brothers and sisters in Christ: A few years ago, I came across the words of the young Jewish intellectual, Etty Hillesum, who was killed in Auschwitz in 1943 at the age of twenty-nine. As she faced the likelihood of deportation and death she wrote that she felt her task was to 'bear witness that God lived' in the terrible circumstances around her. She had to live so as to persuade people that God was real, even in the midst of the horror and insanity of the Nazi era.

> These words still haunt me, because they offer what is surely one of the most authentic and demanding definitions of faith in the modern age. To have faith is to be willing to live so as to show that God is alive. And that means to live in ways which show that there are more possibilities than the world recognises – the possibility of forgiveness, the possibility of reconciliation, the possibility of hope, the possibility of forgetting yourself and being absorbed in the needs of another . . .
>
> The Christmas season reminds us that God created a completely new possibility as Jesus's life on earth began – the possibility of human beings living so fully in intimacy with God through their friendship with Jesus that they come to share something of his own freedom. As you meet and pray and talk, may the possibilities of your lives be opened up, so that you begin to see how, even in the most ordinary of circumstances, you may live in such a way that you show God is alive, and that there is more to the world than anyone could have imagined. I wish you every joy and blessing as you celebrate together the renewal of hope and the enduring life of God in our midst.

This letter was experienced as a kind of mirror, reflecting back to the community something they know they stand for. One of the Brothers I met and spoke to referred to it with real pride. It is not insignificant that both of the Orthodox Patriarchs also commend the work of Taizé. The strained relationships that separate the Churches lose their powerful charge when exposed to the power of the Brothers' work of reconciliation.

This commitment to ecumenism is part of the basic charism of the community. It is recognized as a gift of God given for the benefit of the whole Church, in all its manifestations. For above all the community is ecumenical, and so Catholics and Protestants worship side by side, without drawing attention to the historical and theological divides that have so dominated relationships within the wider Christian community. The richness of both their traditions is reflected in the church's décor, with a Catholic use of light and colour and with Orthodox icons. The focus changes when the Brothers all swing round and stand when the Gospel is read from the Bible, giving supremacy to the word of God at that moment in the true spirit of the Protestant reformation.

The way they handle the Eucharist is significant too, for a Catholic Mass is celebrated daily, before the morning prayer. The morning worship is not eucharistic, though everyone may receive communion at the end, from hosts reserved from the Sunday morning worship. Or else they may take from a basket of unconsecrated bread which is circulated for those who choose to share a sense of community like that.

Another feature that makes the community distinctive is the way in which it is made up of many different nationalities and cultures. This means that the question of language has to be taken seriously.

While French may take pride of place as the native language of the region, there seems to be a general recognition that English is likely to be the first language of many people who go there, or at least the second. On my most recent visit, Finns, Hungarians, Canadians, New Zealanders and Australians swapped experiences happily in English while a lone and rather older French woman was clearly at a disadvantage at table but enjoyed bilingual and trilingual workshops and Bible studies. All the prayer resources and instructions about how to get the most out of the experience of being in Taizé are circulated in at least ten languages. The rubrics are minimal, encouraging people to accept a rhythm dictated by the day's prayer rather than the day's tasks. They include simple instructions about keeping quiet at night, not disturbing people in neighbouring villages and not walking out unaccompanied into the local woods if you are a girl.

The history

So where did the inspiration for this place and experience come from?

One name in particular stands out in the story of Taizé: that of Brother Roger, who founded the community. He was Swiss by birth, the ninth and youngest child of Karl Ulrich Schütz, a Protestant pastor from Bachs in the Zürcher Unterland, and his wife, Amélie Henriette Schütz-Marsauche, a French Protestant woman from Burgundy. He was baptized Roger Louis Schütz-Marsauche in 1915. After studying reformed theology in Strasbourg and Lausanne, he developed TB and had to move to France. He chose the out-of-the-way village of Taizé in his mother's native Burgundy and moved there with his sister Geneviève. This was during World War II, and the village was close to the line of demarcation which separated the part of France occupied by the Germans from the rest.

Young Roger soon began to receive war refugees, including Jews, and for two years he offered them hospitality and shelter. When denounced to the Gestapo, he was able to escape and then returned to Taizé towards the end of the war in 1944 with a small group of Brothers, resolved to live the Christian life in a community 'where simplicity and kind-heartedness would be lived out as essential Gospel realities'. From these small beginnings the group has grown and grown.

Brother Roger himself always avoided the limelight, although his presence was highly charismatic. He wrote copious letters and published books, most notably about prayer. In 1988 he was awarded a UNESCO peace prize. He claimed, 'In reality there is only one true prayer, only one substantial prayer: Christ himself. There is only one voice that rises above the face of the earth: the voice of Christ.' This thoroughly Christocentric focus to his spirituality gave him great clarity and enabled him to make friends outside the magic circle. Those who counted themselves his friends included Pope John Paul II, Mother Teresa and of course the hosts of young people who came to Taizé, where his influence remained constant right up to his death.

Brother Roger's life had a tragic ending when, at the age of 90, he was stabbed to death during evening prayers by a 36-

year-old Romanian woman called Luminita Ruxandra Solcan, in front of a crowd of some 2,500 worshippers in the church at Taizé. She was subsequently diagnosed as a schizophrenic. The date was 16 August 2005.

The violence of that act remains permanently shocking: a man of peace struck down in his own backyard, his own familiar church. What is equally striking is that such a throng of worshippers surrounded him at the time. All of them had gathered to pray that particular August evening and he died as he lived, amid a crowd of friends.

At his funeral, the new Prior of Taizé, Brother Alois, read out this prayer, 'God of goodness, we entrust to your forgiveness Luminita Solcan who, in an act of sickness, put an end to the life of Brother Roger. With Christ on the cross we say to you: Father, forgive her, she does not know what she did.' Not an easy prayer to say, but nevertheless the right one in every sense of the word.

There are now more than 100 Brothers from 25 nations in the community. What is even more significant is that they continue to be from both Catholic and Protestant backgrounds, for Taizé is essentially an ecumenical community. They do not all live in the village. Brothers have gone to all the world's trouble spots, setting up small communities in places as diverse as Belfast and Bangladesh, Senegal and Malawi, Chile and Bolivia – and taking the prayer and work of Taizé wherever they go.

'What Taizé means to me . . .'

Turn to the Internet and you find a wealth of testimonies as people write about their experience of travelling to Taizé. I have chosen two: one by someone who says she struggles to call herself a Christian and yet loves being a follower of Jesus, and one by an ordained minister. Both have something important to say because they testify to the pilgrimage experience.

Before traveling to Taizé, I wrote in one of my papers that Taizé may be like a homecoming for me. Indeed it was very much like that. But it was more mysterious than that. Not like putting on an old pair of beloved shoes kind of homecoming, but like a glimpse of what the ultimate homecoming might be like. It was a little taste of heaven. It is hard to say what exactly led me to the feelings of peace and joy that I bathed in while on the hill of Taizé: stepping away from my life for the first time in eight years, a week without taking care of anyone but myself, the beauty of the prayer times, the gift of silence, the Bible introduction with Brother Emil, the opportunity to talk and talk with people I had only just begun to meet who were also on the same search for the divine, the moments of confession that helped unburden my soul, the personal revelations in communion with the Holy One, the vitamin D that my skin absorbed while sitting, lying, and standing in the beautiful sunlight in the midst of the breathtaking French countryside. Yes, it was all of this, like a spa for my soul, true Sabbath rest. Taizé has not left me, or perhaps more rightly said, I have not fully left Taizé. My physical existence may be thousands of miles away, but my spirit is still receiving blessings and I continue to check the clock wondering if it is prayer time on the other side of the Atlantic. That the brothers are continuing in prayer three times a day is a balm for my soul. Yet Taizé continues with me in my home here in America as well. Once to four, or even five times a week I will slide onto my prayer rug, facing the east, in front of my home altar set with Taizé icons, chalice, and plate, and I will sing. Every chant brings me back to Taizé and that little taste of heaven. The pilgrimage continues . . . (Anon.)

* * *

Taizé. What is Taizé? Music? A worship service? A tiny village in France? Taizé is these things and much more. I first learned of the Taizé style of worship from the Uniting Campus Ministry of Texas Christian University in 1997. I was in seminary at Brite Divinity School and my boyfriend invited me to come to a Taizé service. A sizeable group of students were crammed into the faculty dining room where we had a piano, song sheets and some candles. I liked the music and the serenity of the prayer. I thought it would be exciting to visit Taizé, but didn't think it would ever really happen.

Four years later . . . I became a pilgrim. Pilgrims travel to places of sacred significance to experience the divine in that holy place. Pilgrimage sites of past have been recognized usually for some miraculous occurrence, association with prophets, saints, or the death of a martyr. In more modern usage, pilgrimage sites have come to include places more loosely defined as sacred or divinely significant; places where one expects to encounter God. But pilgrimage isn't just about the destination; it's about the journey. Like walking a labyrinth is not about what happens in the center; it's about the entire process of moving to the center and back out again.

So thirteen of us turned up at Cincinnati airport on the first of June and our pilgrim paths joined. We were excited about experiencing something new. Only our leader, Guy McCombs, had been to Taizé before. We arrived at Taizé on Pentecost Sunday. The majority of our fellow international pilgrims would not arrive until Monday, though the usual 'meeting' runs Sunday to Sunday.

Quickly we were taken into the life of the community. The young adults of the group were given options as to how we would spend our week. We could concentrate on Bible study and discussion in small groups, or we could work a job and have a shorter time of study and discussion. Most of us chose the work and study route, which involved the usual chores of clean-up (all kinds), cooking, welcoming and generally helping life go on.

Our study groups met once a day and we had a mix of Americans, Germans, a French Canadian, a Swiss, and a Pole. It was difficult at first, because most everything had to be translated for the other members of the group. This greatly limited our ability to bond swiftly, but by the end of the week we were beginning to gel. We also bonded with our work groups; mine tended to have more English speakers who came from Ireland and Germany. It made me mindful of how we are so spoiled to live in the USA where 99 per cent of the time or better we can operate in one language.

Then there is the prayer. Three times each day, morning, noon and evening, the bells ring out and call the entire community to prayer. Everything else stops and the focus is on God. To describe the church and the prayer service does not do it justice, but imagine if you can an expandable sanctuary, which this week held 1,500–2,000 people each time. We are all Christians, whether Roman Catholic, Protestant or Orthodox. Our fellow pilgrims spoke German, French, Italian, English in a variety of accents, Polish, Russian, Swedish and more. The largest nationality represented was German. Scriptures and prayers are read in several of the represented languages, and the songs are sung in the same variety.

It really did seem like Pentecost each time we gathered for prayer because each person heard or sang something in her or his own language. On Monday when we sang, 'In the Lord I'll be Ever Thankful' in German, it was awesome to behold. It was like the scene in *The Sound of Music* when the Von Trapps start to sing 'Edelweiss' and the entire crowd joins in. The music is exponentially louder and ever more expressive because it is sung from the heart. It literally brought tears to my eyes and made that song one of my favorites. I'm still singing it in German even though I also know the words in English.

And then there is the silence. Each prayer service includes a time of silence – usually about five minutes at the morning and noonday prayer and about ten minutes at evening prayer. For some, even five minutes seemed an eternity of discomfort and uneasiness, especially when accompanied by an eagerness to get to breakfast or lunch. But for me, it never seemed enough. For those who tend towards introversion or contemplativeness it is blessed silence that melts away too quickly like the last of a favorite candy savored in the mouth. It only leaves you wanting more.

In this short space I can only hope to have given you glimpses of the community at Taizé. I can tell you it is not something you can go and see in an hour or a day like a painting or a statue; it is alive and must be experienced to be understood and appreciated. Taizé is not a movement, a style of worship or a new denomination; it is a way of living out the gospel in community. The brothers will tell you that what happens away from Taizé, what we in the USA call Taizé worship, is 'worship with the songs of Taizé'. What Taizé would have us take home is the reconciliation of all Christians for the unity of the Body of Christ. This mission is a divinely mandated, intentional habit that requires cultivation. Most importantly, it cannot be done alone.

(The Revd Carolyn Roper-Fowlkes,
reproduced with permission)

Some exercises to help you pray in the spirit of Taizé

1 Read Luke 10.25–37 reflectively then think about these questions and see if you can answer them:

- Why does Jesus answer the law expert's questions with a question?
- Which people living near me show great generosity to others?
- What place do others have in my life? How important to me are their desires and needs?
- What barriers keep us from going towards others? How can we surmount these barriers?
- How do we reply to those who say, 'I don't know what to do with my life'? (© Taizé)

Then read Luke 18.31–34 and see how Jesus himself takes the place of the man who fell among thieves.

These questions come from a Taizé Bible study.

2 Buy yourself a CD of some of the Taizé chants and sing along with them as you set aside time for prayer, or go to <www.taize.fr/en_article681.html> to download a podcast of Taizé worship.

3 Make the pilgrimage yourself. Go to Taizé. Look online at the travel directions given at <www.taize.fr/en_rubrique18.html> and book yourself in.

7

Redemption Song

Singing and praying

'Whoever sings prays twice.' These words, attributed to St Augustine of Hippo, an early fourth-century Church Father, are beloved of all church musicians, whether at Taizé or in a cathedral organ-loft or at your local parish church. After all, the idea sanctions their work: it is encouraging to think that every time you sing in God's praise, you are praying twice over. Augustine was writing about the Psalms, the collection of Old Testament hymns that give glory to God and thanksgiving for the great work of redemption. So Christianity did not invent the tradition of using singing this way. Music in all its forms, either singing to God or playing instruments in his service, are as integral to the Jewish faith as they are to Christianity. Indeed, to understand the need to sing – and so to praise God twice – we need to go back to the Hebrew Scriptures to understand the origins of church music.

The Old Testament

Historians of musical instruments are sometimes baffled by the lists they find in the pages of the Hebrew Scriptures. The exultant words of Psalm 57.8, 'Awake, my soul! Awake, O harp and lyre! I will awake the dawn', give a simple list combining harps and lyres, both of which have their present-day equivalents, so that we can imagine the sound they would have made. But other lists are less easy to unravel: 'the sound of the horn, pipe, lyre, trigon, harp and bagpipe' for example, as cited in Daniel 3.15, is depicted as alien music, as used by the king Nebuchadnezzar. A trigon is a three-sided lyre, so the sound would have been a combination of brass, strings and woodwind playing in an unknown key to unknown rhythms. Yet whatever the sound, the association is clear enough: music – even when used by foreigners – is about celebration. Music honours God and so does song. Indeed, one of the most poignant of all the psalms shows us this clearly. From his place of exile beside the river Chebar, the psalmist reflects:

> By the waters of Babylon,
> there we sat down and wept,
> when we remembered Zion.
> On the willows there
> we hung up our lyres.
> For there our captors
> required of us songs,
> and our tormentors, mirth, saying,
> 'Sing us one of the songs of Zion!'
> How shall we sing the LORD's song
> in a foreign land?
> (Psalm 137.1–4, RSV)

Hanging up your harp is tantamount to giving up, so the idea of 'no music' and 'no song' becomes an image of despair. Contrariwise, music and song are synonymous with the praise of God.

So who are the Old Testament musicians and when do they play? We know some of them by name. Miriam, for instance, the sister of Moses (who led the chosen people out of Egypt towards the freedom of the Promised Land) is a name to conjure with. In Exodus we read,

> Then Miriam, the prophetess, the sister of [Moses and] Aaron, took a timbrel in her hand; and all the women went out after her with timbrels and dancing. And Miriam sang to them:
>
> 'Sing to the Lord, for he has triumphed gloriously;
> the horse and his rider he has thrown into the sea.'
>
> (Exodus 15.20–22, RSV)

This is a high point in the development of Israelite self-consciousness, the moment of Exodus, an event which is still recalled at the feast of Passover. And it has music at its heart. The great canticle of praise, or Miriam's song, is recited in Christian celebrations of the resurrection of Jesus as well, because it has its natural place during the Easter Midnight Mass, celebrating his exodus from death to life.

Another named musician is King David, who sang in front of the Ark of the Covenant as it was brought on a cart down to the Holy City where, eventually, the Temple would be built. The sound is evoked by associating merriment and might with a galaxy of noisy instruments: 'And David and all the house of Israel were making merry before the Lord with all their might, with songs and lyres and harps and tambourines and castanets and cymbals' (2 Samuel 6.5, RSV). When his descendant, Solomon, both built and consecrated the Temple, more musicians are mentioned by name, as well as the astonishing sound they must have made:

> Now when the priests came out of the holy place (for all the priests who were present had sanctified themselves, without regard to their divisions; and all the Levitical singers, Asaph, Heman, and Jedu'thun, their sons and kinsmen, arrayed in fine linen, with cymbals, harps, and lyres, stood east of the altar with a hundred and twenty priests who were trumpeters; and it was the duty of the trumpeters and singers to make themselves heard in unison in praise and thanksgiving to the Lord), and when the song was raised, with trumpets and cymbals and other musical instruments, in praise to the Lord,

> 'For he is good,
> for his steadfast love endures for ever,'
>
> the house, the house of the LORD, was filled with a cloud, so that the priests could not stand to minister because of the cloud; for the glory of the LORD filled the house of God.
>
> (2 Chronicles 5.11–14, RSV)

This time the sound of sacred music is coupled with glory as God's presence fills the Temple in the form of a great cloud.

The inferences are clear: that music is for everyone, man, woman, king, prophet, priest; that music is fun – more raucous than reverential; and of course that it generates some powerful lyrics. Some of these have been captured in the set-piece, one-off songs that are sung by Hannah, for instance, when she first presents her boy for service in the Temple, under the prophet Eli. This is the future prophet Samuel.

> Hannah also prayed and said,
> 'My heart exults in the LORD;
> my strength is exalted in the LORD.
> My mouth derides my enemies,
> because I rejoice in thy salvation.
>
> There is none holy like the LORD,
> there is none besides thee;
> there is no rock like our God.'
>
> (1 Samuel 2.1–2, RSV)

The tone is exultant but also, we are reassured, Hannah is both singing and praying. This is the note struck by the psalms, which are at once songs of praise and acts of prayer. No wonder so many of them have been set to music so effectively; no wonder the sound of plainsong in a Catholic church or that of metered psalms at Anglican Evensong offers us a spiritual experience in its own right.

And what about the themes of Old Testament songs? In Bob Marley's words they are essentially redemption songs. The great Jamaican wrote of the slavery of his people taken from

Africa to serve on the sugar plantations of the Caribbean, and used scriptural themes to explain what this meant. By comparing their experience to that of the Israelites he found a new symbolic meaning for a meaningless act of brutality and exploitation, and openly alluded to its redemptive quality. The most celebrated of his lyrics, 'Redemption Song', opens by remembering the historical facts and then makes the connection. His hand, he claims, was made strong because God became his saviour.

Yet he is realistic as well, for beyond the physical slavery of the African experience there lurks a deeper slavery that has us all in its grip. So great is our common need for freedom that no one can pretend that this scriptural message is not for them. Marley sings about emancipation from mental slavery, saying that we have to free our minds from it for our songs to become true 'songs of freedom'.

Similarly with his lyrics for 'Exodus': he captures the reality both of slavery (which he calls Babylon) and of the freedom which lies ahead by asking if we are satisfied with life as it is or if we aspire to move on, to go to a different place – which he calls our fatherland. Again the message is clear: what is needed is self-knowledge and self-appraisal. Redemption is not about then, some time in the past which is over, dead and buried; redemption is about now and it is something we all crave. The redemption tradition has formed an integral part of blues singing and of jazz. No wonder it made the leap over to popular music in such a telling way at the hands of Bob Marley. He ensured that it should not be lost or consigned to the hymnbooks.

The New Testament

Move to the New Testament and there are plenty of references to the musical activities of the early Church, yet the word music is strangely absent from the four Gospels. Luke alone uses it when he tells us that the older brother in the parable of the prodigal son was annoyed when he came home from the fields and heard the sound of 'music and dancing', indicating that his brother had returned and that his father was celebrating with a party. Yet the theme of celebration is constant and reflected in the gathering of early Christians who assembled to sing God's praises and, increasingly, to partake in the great act of thanksgiving they came to call the Eucharist.

In Colossians 3.16 we read of Paul telling the people to 'Let the word of Christ dwell in you richly, teach and admonish one another in all wisdom, and sing psalms and hymns and spiritual songs with thankfulness in your hearts to God' (RSV). So he writes of psalms, meaning the legacy the Christian people has inherited from the Hebrew Scriptures; he then separates out hymns and sacred songs, though the difference between the two must be a matter of conjecture. The point is that Christianity itself had now generated its own repertoire of sacred music. This insight is repeated in Ephesians, where we read that the people are to 'be filled with the Spirit, addressing one another in psalms and hymns and spiritual songs, singing and making melody to the Lord with all your heart, always and for everything giving thanks in the name of our Lord Jesus Christ to God the Father' (Ephesians 5.18–20, RSV). Once again, thanksgiving is linked to song, music to celebration.

Luke alone gives us the story of the prodigal son, with its passing reference to music, and to Luke too we owe all the great canticles or hymns of the New Testament. Most of them are associated with his accounts of the birth of Jesus. So to start with we have the Magnificat, the song of Mary when she greets her cousin Elizabeth in Luke 1.46–55. The two women are both pregnant, and John the Baptist's mother, Elizabeth, feels her baby recognize the coming saviour. As she says, 'the child in my womb leapt for joy'. This same joy inspires Mary's words. 'My soul magnifies the Lord,' she says, echoing the song of Hannah from 1 Samuel 2. She then goes on to proclaim a new dispensation where all earthly values will be reversed and the poor shall inherit the land, the hungry be filled, while the rich and mighty are sent empty away. The kingdom of God is first proclaimed by Mary in this exultant song and prayer.

When John the Baptist is born, his father Zechariah too assumes a prophetic mantle and breaks into song. He blesses and praises God who has, he claims, both 'visited and redeemed his people' by raising up 'a horn of salvation for us in the house of his servant David' (Luke 1.68–69, RSV). The language of the Benedictus – 'Blessed be the Lord God of Israel, for he has visited and redeemed his people' – may be that of the Old Testament but, once again, the sentiments are those of the New. Zechariah's perspective is on the future as he predicts his son's role in the economy of salvation:

> And you, child, will be called the prophet of the Most High;
> for you will go before the Lord to prepare his ways,
> to give knowledge of salvation to his people
> in the forgiveness of their sins,
> through the tender mercy of our God,
> when the day shall dawn upon us from on high
> to give light to those who sit in darkness and in the shadow
> of death,
> to guide our feet into the way of peace.
>
> (Luke 1.76–79, RSV)

The great daybreak 'from on high' is the moment of the nativity of Jesus, and here again song comes into its own. Luke tells us that the multitude of the heavenly host themselves were already joined in the hymn of all creation when they appeared to shepherds on the hills above Bethlehem to sing, 'Glory to God in the highest, and on earth peace among men with whom he is pleased!' (Luke 2.14, RSV). This refrain has been translated into Christian liturgy as the Gloria. So too with the next of Luke's great canticles, for the Nunc Dimittis is also part of his Gospel's narrative. Another old man, Simeon, is at his daily work in the Temple when Jesus' parents bring the boy in 'to do for him according to the custom of the law'. He takes the child in his arms and proclaims that he is now ready to die, because he has seen the saviour of his people.

> Lord, now lettest thou thy servant depart in peace,
> according to thy word;
> for mine eyes have seen thy salvation
> which thou hast prepared in the presence of all peoples,
> a light for revelation to the Gentiles,
> and for glory to thy people Israel.
>
> (Luke 2.29–32, RSV)

To a certain extent these four great canticles are so familiar that we take them for granted, because they are integral to Christian liturgical practice. Yet this should not mask their extreme antiquity and the practice they represent. From them we learn that the early Christian community was both a praying community and a singing community. The holy people from the Scriptures who recognized the importance of the birth of Jesus can help us praise and recognize him in our turn when we choose to pray and sing their words.

A living tradition

No surprise then that at each age in the Church's history new music, new lyrics and new inspiration have been called forth in God's praise. The tradition of Church music is alive and well and flourishing. So what makes for a good hymn or redemption song? We all have our own favourites, and the idea of laying down criteria may seem alien to some. But there are certain guidelines that can help us identify the best hymn writers and get more out of singing their hymns.

Which hymns can help us to 'pray twice'? A good tune always helps – and the best, such as 'Abide with Me' and 'Guide

Me, O Thou Great Jehovah' have travelled successfully from their religious roots to the secular world of the football or rugby stadium in a seamless trajectory. Many of the 'best' hymns have more than one tune for that very reason. The musicians who are attracted to them want to write the definitive tune, to get the best match between tune and lyrics.

In this way we aspire to join with the hymns of the angels. As we have already seen, when the Church sings it joins its voice to a melody that is already being sung. When the shepherds were abiding in the fields and watching their flocks by night, the veil between heaven and earth was momentarily lifted. They saw and heard the angelic song which is ceaselessly offered to God and they became part of it. That is what happens to us when we sing God's praises: our voices are joined to those of the angels. The writer of one of the most ancient of the Church's hymns put this idea into words when he wrote his hymn, 'Let All Mortal Flesh Keep Silence'. The first words are based on a text from an Old Testament prophet, 'Let all the earth keep silence before him' (Habakkuk 2.20, RSV), and they advocate silence. Why should a hymn start with a plea for silence? The reason becomes clear in the third and fourth verses of this ancient hymn, which is preserved for us in a fifth-century collection attributed to St James. We are to keep silence so that we can hear the other music, the angels' music, and join in with it.

Rank on rank the host of heaven
Spreads its vanguard on the way,
As the Light of light descendeth
From the realms of endless day,
That the powers of hell may vanish
As the darkness clears away.

At His feet the six-winged seraph;
Cherubim with sleepless eye,
Veil their faces to the Presence,

As with ceaseless voice they cry,
Alleluya, Alleluya,
Alleluya, Lord most high!

We sing along with angels. That is how our song becomes a double prayer and why musicians rise to the challenge of hymn writing. The words or lyrics are important too because they hold the hopes and aspirations of every human heart. In Old Testament times, as we have seen, hymns and psalms fulfilled a double purpose. They were there to help people praise God and they celebrated redemption, the idea that God intervenes in the lives of his people and seeks to lead us out of slavery and captivity into freedom. The best hymns follow that twofold pattern as well.

Take a genuinely 'classical' hymn, one that bridges every part of the Christian tradition, whether Catholic or Protestant, ancient or modern. The one I want to choose is 'Praise to the Holiest in the Height'. The words were written by John Henry Newman in 1865, when he was aged 64. He had been an Anglican priest until his conversion to Roman Catholicism some 20 years previously. The hymn was part of his extended poem *The Dream of Gerontius*. In 1900, the British composer Edward Elgar would set the whole poem to music in the form of an oratorio, ensuring that this amazing hymn would never be forgotten. In the oratorio, the words are sung by the angels of the heavenly host as they give praise for the life of Jesus and his work of redemption. The two themes of praise and redemption are brought together in a balanced and elegant whole as we in our turn sing with them,

Praise to the Holiest in the height,
And in the depth be praise;
In all His words most wonderful,
Most sure in all His ways.

O loving wisdom of our God!
When all was sin and shame,

A second Adam to the fight
And to the rescue came.

O wisest love! that flesh and blood,
Which did in Adam fail,
Should strive afresh against the foe,
Should strive and should prevail.

And that a higher gift than grace
Should flesh and blood refine,
God's Presence and His very Self,
And Essence all divine.

O generous love! that He, who smote,
In Man for man the foe,
The double agony in Man
For man should undergo.

And in the garden secretly,
And on the Cross on high,
Should teach His brethren, and inspire
To suffer and to die.

Praise to the Holiest in the height,
And in the depth be praise;
In all His words most wonderful,
Most sure in all His ways.

That hymn would be a hard act to follow, largely because of the confidence with which it asserts that God is 'wonderful' and 'sure in all his ways'. It comes from a praying heart, from the mind of a man who has experienced the sure touch of God on his life and rejoices in it. It is realistic about suffering and about its redemptive quality; it brings us into the presence of God and assures us that in the gift of the incarnation we have a 'higher gift than grace'. The birth of Jesus brings God's very essence to us and his death on the cross defeats all defeat and sets us free.

The solid theological core of Newman's hymn sets it apart beyond its qualities as a poetic masterpiece. And poetry in hymns is a quality that ensures that some are promised a place in every hymnbook. The language may be quaint or dated, but who can refuse a place to words by poets such as George Herbert or Charles Wesley? Herbert wrote his 'King of Glory, King of Peace' in 1633 when the Church and world were at anything but peace.

King of glory, King of peace,
I will love thee;
and that love may never cease,
I will move thee.
Thou hast granted my request,
thou hast heard me;
thou didst note my working breast,
thou hast spared me.

Wherefore with my utmost art
I will sing thee,
and the cream of all my heart
I will bring thee.
Though my sins against me cried,
thou didst clear me;
and alone, when they replied,
thou didst hear me.

Seven whole days, not one in seven,
I will praise thee;
in my heart, though not in heaven,
I can raise thee.
Small it is, in this poor sort
to enrol thee:
e'en eternity's too short
to extol thee.

The conceit works, for Herbert's poem in praise of love overrides all concerns about his sins and ensures that God is praised not simply on Sunday but every day. He offers the very best of himself, the 'cream' of his heart, and finds that time itself fails him because it is not long enough to sustain all the praise due to God. The poet's worship becomes a prayer.

Charles Wesley

The greatest hymn writer of them all was Charles Wesley. We go to a Newman for theological content and clarity, to a Herbert for lyricism and poetry, but for the soul of British hymnody we need the inspiration of Wesley. For he combines theology with lyricism with profound devotion. All the warmth of a clear head and a loving heart are combined in his verses. Born in 1707, so neatly spanning the generations between Herbert and Newman, Charles and his older brother John were ordained in the Church of England before making a break with it and joining others to form the Methodist movement and Church. They first associated with a group known as the Oxford Methodists, united by their evangelical love of Christ and the Scriptures which they studied and applied to their lives with methodical discipline. They were good, upright people, men of the Book who embraced poverty with a diligent love of the poor and care for the needs of others. Both brothers were prolific preachers and hymn writers, but Charles' work is remembered for its staunch devotion and living piety. No hymn captures his devotion so well as 'And Can it Be?' The tone is autobiographical as Charles remembers the moment on 21 May 1738 when he received the overwhelming experience of grace that turned his life around and enabled him to believe that he had indeed gained 'an interest in his Saviour's blood', namely that he was redeemed.

And can it be that I should gain
An interest in the Saviour's blood?
Died He, for me, who caused His pain
For me, who Him to death pursued?
Amazing love! How can it be

That thou, my God, shouldst die for me?
Amazing love! How can it be
That thou, my God, shouldst die for me?

'Tis mystery all! th' Immortal dies:
Who can explore His strange design?
In vain the firstborn seraph tries
To sound the depths of love divine.
'Tis mercy all! Let earth adore;
Let angel minds inquire no more.
'Tis mercy all! Let earth adore;
Let angel minds inquire no more.

He left His Father's throne above
So free, so infinite his grace!
Emptied Himself of all but love,
And bled for Adam's helpless race.
'Tis mercy all, immense and free;
For, O my God, it found out me!
'Tis mercy all, immense and free,
For, O my God, it found out me!

Long my imprisoned sprit lay,
Fast bound in sin and nature's night;
Thine eye diffused a quickening ray,
I woke, the dungeon flamed with light;
My chains fell off, my heart was free,
I rose, went forth, and followed Thee.
My chains fell off, my heart was free,
I rose, went forth, and followed Thee.

Still the small inward voice I hear,
That whispers all my sins forgiven;
Still the atoning blood is near,
That quenched the wrath of hostile Heaven.
I feel the life His wounds impart;
I feel the Saviour in my heart.
I feel the life His wounds impart;
I feel the Saviour in my heart.

No condemnation now I dread;
Jesus, and all in Him, is mine!
Alive in Him, my living Head,
And clothed in righteousness divine,
Bold I approach the eternal throne,
And claim the crown, through Christ my own.
Bold I approach the eternal throne,
And claim the crown, through Christ my own.

The text on which this narrative hymn is based comes from Acts 12.7, where we read an account of the imprisonment of the apostle Peter. In the middle of the night his prison cell blazes with light because an angel visits him to set him free: 'The angel of the Lord appeared, and a light shone in the cell; and he struck Peter on the side, and woke him, saying, 'Get up quickly.' And the chains fell off his hands' (RSV). No image captures the sensation of freedom experienced by someone who turns to Jesus in complete faith so powerfully as this. The hymn is a testament to the workings of grace.

Yet in reality it does illustrate a common problem we have nowadays with some of the imagery that helped previous generations. For without question or doubt, the hymn uses the language of blood and redemption in ways some find unpalatable. When I first gave a retreat to Methodist students I was delighted when a group of them decided to dramatize this hymn. Spoken slowly, either by one individual representing Wesley/Peter or by a chorus representing a crowd of believers, it made a marvellous impression. Except did it? Later that evening one of the young Methodist trainee ministers said to me that he found the whole thing unsingable, and precisely because of its imagery. He could not bear the reference to blood or the idea of having an interest or investment in it. We talked at length, with me making a passionate defence of his Methodist heritage and the student telling me he was prepared to sacrifice that to his sense of integrity. What mattered to him was that singing about blood sounded gory. The dilemma remained unresolved, but the irony of the situation struck me.

For many congregations nowadays have given up on singing the classic hymns, preferring to go for choruses where words of praise are repeated over and over again and where there is little theological or even scriptural content. Both Charles and John Wesley would be astonished at our failure of nerve, I believe. A good hymn, sung by a devout congregation, unites heaven and earth in God's praise. We do indeed sing along with angels.

Some exercises to help you sing and 'pray twice'

1 Choose your favourite hymn and decide why you like it so much. Is it the association with the time you first sang it? Is it because of the words? See if you can buy a CD compilation with it on and play it in the car.
2 Pretend that you are responsible for choosing all the hymns for your own funeral. If you are able to, discuss this with other family members. After all, they are the ones who are going to be singing them without you. Talk about your choices and explain what they mean to you so that these memories can be shared later. Write a letter to go alongside your will, with all your choices noted down.
3 Write the first verse of a brand-new hymn to the tune of one you already know. Then see if you feel tempted to continue. Many congregations have shared cookery or recipe books. Why not a shared hymn book with old favourites and some of your own hymns for yours?

8

'And the Word was made flesh'

Art and religion

Just as music and religion have produced a powerful fusion and spiritual culture, so too art and religion come together to help Christians pray. We use art to adorn our churches and our homes because of our need to open a window onto the divine. Pictures are able to do that for us, and so too are stained glass, carved stone, ceramics, statues and all manner of artefacts, because the human heart is uplifted by beauty. Beyond words – even at their most sacred; beyond music even, there is a world waiting to be explored when we open our imaginations to art. It is not by chance that the calling of an artist is described as a vocation, for their task is to engage with the activity of God, the first artist and original creator of all that is. What God began, they continue.

The artistic tradition of the west demonstrates something fundamental to our self-understanding: for Christianity is able to accommodate the idea that God can be represented and also that representations of the Trinity, of Jesus in his humanity, of Mary, the angels and saints make up a major part of a shared inheritance and culture. We take this for granted. For Judaism and Islam the opposite holds good: God cannot and must not be depicted. Why is this?

The Ten Commandments given by God to Moses on Mount Sinai state expressly that believers are not to use graven images to try to depict God.

> I am the LORD, your God . . . you shall have no other gods before me.
>
> You shall not make for yourself a graven image, or any likeness of anything that is in heaven above, or that is in the earth beneath, or that is in the water under the earth; you shall not bow down to them or serve them; for I the LORD your God am a jealous God . . . (Exodus 20.2–5, RSV)

Nothing is to be depicted that might be worshipped in the place of God. So in accordance with the prohibition, the greatest of Jewish artists, such as Marc Chagall, aim at something that is non-representational when they produce sacred art. His 12 'stained-glass windows' at the Abbell Synagogue in Jerusalem's university hospital at Hadassah seem to float through the air as they evoke for us Jacob's blessing of his 12 sons and Moses' of the 12 tribes of Israel. Animals, fish and flowers compete to catch the eye, combining brilliant colour and light to give glory to God and inspire the believer to prayer. These windows convey a sense of the sacred – and that is what religious art is all about – but they still do this within the understanding set out by the second commandment.

Islam is equally clear in its condemnation of representation and for an equally deeply held theological reason. The western world associates Islamic religious art with the architectural glories of such mosques as the Great Umayyad mosque of Damascus or that of the Hagia Sophia basilica of Istanbul. Calligraphy too, because it is not pictorial, has flourished in a culture that has high regard for form and line, especially when used to embellish copies of the Qur'an. Most familiar of all is the tradition of carpet making. Oriental rugs have brought Islamic art right into the homes of people outside of the Muslim world, and many of us are unaware that the antique rugs – or their modern reproductions – that adorn our homes may once have served as prayer mats. The telltale signs are the orientation of the patterns, all designed to act as arrows, so that the rugs can be lined up to point towards Mecca. The sheer unfamiliarity of Muslim culture means that its religious inspiration can be hard for Christians to decipher, but that is no reason not to appreciate the deep spiritual impulse which led to the development of Islamic art. If anything, the prohibition on depicting God or his angels and saints has led to a proliferation of the symbolic on a scale that exceeds anything achieved in the west.

At the heart of the Christian imagination lies the belief that the Word became flesh; the understanding that God chose to be depicted in human form. So that not only are all humans made in the divine image and likeness, but in the person of Jesus in particular, God actually appeared among us. It follows that material things can become a real presence, conveying God to us, just as the human body and blood and the Eucharistic body and blood of Jesus do. To represent images of Bible stories or what can loosely be called religious art becomes a spiritual activity and one of Christianity's glories. This means that when we go to a cathedral or church or museum, we take it for granted that we will see things that try to tell us what God is like and how we can react to what we see. We are visually aware, and that is part of our cultural as well as spiritual experience. A couple shown, usually weeping, with an apple and a snake become Adam and Eve, who equal our first parents/the Fall/eviction from the Garden of Eden. Another couple, the woman heavily pregnant, the man leading a donkey, become Mary and Joseph making their way to Bethlehem for the birth of Jesus/the Incarnation/the dawn of our redemption – and so on. We are used to the idea that pictures tell stories and that they can feed our spiritual life and help us pray.

This was not always the case. In the eighth century, early Christian art in the Byzantine empire came under fire. For theologians and lay people alike began to question the value of making things that could not possibly share the same matter with what they sought to represent. The Byzantine emperor, Leo III, who was a Syrian, joined his support to theirs. No amount of gold or silver, of wood or stone could represent the Godhead, these critics reckoned. So works of art should be broken up. You can see an example of iconoclasm at St George's monastery in Mabada in Jordan. On the church floor is a mosaic map of the Holy Land. In the hinterland above the river Jordan, a lion is shown chasing a hind. So far so good; only the lion has no real body. To use a modern term, it has been pixelated out. That is to say, the mosaic pieces have been removed and reassembled in a random order so that the outline of the lion's body has gone. Only its tail remains intact. A small example, but one that reminds us how thorough the work of destruction could have been.

In the event the western Christians won out as they had fewer scruples about representation. After all, the western Church had no particular interest in trying to accommodate the growing influence of Islam, or to learn from it. So while eastern theologians such as John of Damascus began to condemn icons and iconography, Christians in the former Roman world of the Mediterranean and all points west saw no problem with them. The matter was resolved in their favour but, as we shall see, the issue went underground for a while and it would reappear later, at the time of the Reformation.

Icons survived and iconic art flourished, especially in the Orthodox world. What is an icon and why are they so revered? We all have icons; they fill our computer screens, so we are familiar with the idea that one thing, in this case a little thumbnail picture, can point to another of far greater importance. Double-click on a blue letter 'W' and the whole world of Microsoft Word opens up for you, for instance. That is what the original religious icons were intended to do – to open up hidden worlds to us. Only in their case, the worlds were real; that is to say, insubstantial but true: the world of heaven, if you like, with God, the Virgin Mary and the angels and saints lined up before us.

Icon painters pray before they set to work. They dedicate their skill and their task to God because they know that they are not seeking personal glory, rather they are trying to open religious meaning for us. Each individual painting, each individual brush stroke gives a perspective onto God. Some of the earliest icons in the Christian tradition have even been attributed to St Luke, the Gospel writer. He is alleged to have painted Mary the mother of Jesus. The oldest icon of Christ himself is preserved at St Catherine's monastery on Mount Sinai in Egypt, and is known as the *Pantocrator*, or *All-Powerful Christ*. None of these images claims to be an exact likeness, because that would be to miss the point. An icon is a representation, not a photograph. Its purpose is to help us pray, so arguably it is religious art at its purest.

How do you pray with an icon? First, by allowing yourself to be swept up into the idea that this image is a threshold, a gateway. You stand before it and knock. That is to say, you allow yourself space and time to be composed and silent in the presence of a mystery and gradually the icon opens and reveals its mysteries to you. It becomes a portal and you walk over the threshold in your imagination and are drawn into the contemplation of things unseen. This needs time and a willingness to experience the unfamiliar.

Many churches these days have quiet corners where it is possible to withdraw in the presence of an icon and spend time in silence. Alternatively you can go online and save one to your computer screen. For example, a visit to <http://touregypt.net/featurestories/catherines2.htm> is a good starting point. Right-click on the icon of your choice and save it to your screen. Let it become your 'Icon of icons'.

The golden age of Christian art

More familiar to the western imagination is the art of Europe's golden age. So cast your mind back a thousand years and what do we have? A culture that was dominated by Christianity and its values. What does this mean for art in general, and for public art in particular? Religion supplied opportunities for artists. It was, in essence, a benefactor and its influence was benign. The great themes of religious art were given by the Bible. So we have mothers and babies, because of the high place granted to the Madonna with her child, as well as other stories of ordinary people, all used to illustrate events from the life, death and resurrection of Jesus. He calls fishermen by the seashore, he preaches to a crowd on a mountain top, he dies graphically on a cross, he rises in glory and is depicted meeting Mary Magdalene in the garden or a doubting Thomas in the upper room.

Nature, interiors; men, women, children; human hopes and expectations, as well as grief and doubt, pain and joy; bread, wine, grapes, figs; oxen and asses; agony, passion, love, life, death. All the great themes of human life – and consequently of art – are here.

The Old Testament or Hebrew Scriptures also gave an imaginative range of different scenes to inspire artists: an angel prevents Abraham from slaughtering his child, Moses comes down from Mount Sinai bearing the commandments on tablets of stone, David confronts Goliath. Patriarchs, prophets and kings parade for us in frescoes and tapestries as well as in paintings and sculptures. Then there are symbolic actions as nature collaborates in the work of grace, such as the parting of the Red Sea, the gift of manna and quails in the wilderness, the ravens who feed Elijah, the plant that withers over the prophet Jonah. From Church history too we have further imagery, with saints, such as Catherine with her wheel, Agatha with her breasts on a plate, Christopher with the child Jesus on his back. An age that valued the imagination and visual imagery gave an abundance of inspiration to its artists and craftsmen. It also produced the money to employ them and rewarded their work with celebrity and further work.

For if the Bible and the story of the early Christian community supplied the imagery, the Church itself supplied benefaction and patronage by building churches and cathedrals and stuffing them with what became known as religious art. Craftsmen whose names we will never know wandered all over Europe creating an immense range of buildings and artefacts. In addition, an army of monks and scholars laboured over manuscripts, creating illustrated copies of the Bible on vellum. Imagine the monk who created the 'Book of Kells', carefully choosing his squirrel-hair brushes, selecting his paints and setting out to create a masterpiece. You can see the results in Trinity College Library in Dublin: a magnificent creation, with monsters and demons, angels and saints in abundance, all decorating and illustrating his text.

Or come to Wells in Somerset where I live and you will see the largest collection of sculpture in Europe on the façade of its Gothic cathedral. The masons and craftsmen who worked there travelled light, packing their hammers and trowels and journeying on to further glories all over Europe. Or go to Notre Dame in Paris or Chartres cathedral and be bowled over by the stained glass – a visual feast for everyone to enjoy.

It was, if you like, a golden age for artists, craftsmen and for the faithful as well, because they could live and move and have their being in large public spaces adorned for their edification and benefit. Their spirits were invited to breathe through exposure to beauty and to art of the highest order. So what happened next?

The new iconoclasm

The Reformation: and so a death knell for public art, with the triumph of the word over the picture, a text to be read rather than an imaginative world to be touched and tasted and smelt and enjoyed. By focusing attention on the Bible as divine revelation to be interpreted and understood, rather than as a treasure house to be raided for pictures and stories, it could be argued that the Protestant churches deliberately stifled the visual arts. Even their emphasis on grace rather than works, namely the idea that faith alone justifies us, serves to undermine the value of art. For a playful sharing in the creative work of God – the very spirit that enabled religious art to flourish – was condemned by the more extreme forms of Protestantism. At its most Puritan, the movement outlawed colour too, in the name of plainness and simplicity. And how do you depict grace at work in the world without line and form and colour?

So look more closely at the west front of my home cathedral at Wells and there is critical evidence of what the Puritans did. They defaced the art by knocking the heads off all the lowest statues – the ones they could reach easily – and broke the stained glass windows. In smaller churches they removed the glass and painted over the wall frescoes with cool white limestone paint. The treasury of church architecture was vandalized in the name of submission to the word, and the artists and craftsmen were disempowered as the printing presses began to roll, producing Bibles for the masses. Reading became valued more than looking; the life of the spirit was put on hold as the mind and heart took over.

Yet nature abhors a vacuum and the human spirit cannot be crushed in such an abject way without demanding revenge. So in the artistic world we have the birth of the baroque, the excesses of rococo. This was accompanied by the privatization of public art as it became the possession of a rich elite for the expression of their personal wealth, rather than of illiterate people for whom it had been free, provided for the glory of God rather than for the glory of individuals and their families.

In Catholic countries, such as Austria, Spain, Portugal, France and south Germany, religious artefacts went on being produced and the flame of earlier religious inspiration continued to flourish. This is not to say that all the art was beautiful, but at least the idea of depiction was not outlawed. After all, if you think about it, the Christian Bible does not sanction such an attitude. Christianity was never meant to be like that. At their best, art and religion were never intended to be enemies. Rather art was a friend to the gospel – and vice versa.

Art and prayer

Why is all this important? The earliest religious artists knew instinctively that there is a direct route from the eye to the human heart; from a work of art to the human soul. That is why art helps us pray. That is why church buildings were to be decorated. Their overt purpose may have been to give glory to God by producing objects of beauty but their real rationale went deeper than that. From the unseen and unknown world of the human imagination, they could conjure up images that would feed the life of the spirit simply by being there. Things could nurture the life of prayer.

This happens on a personal level. As individuals we respond to beauty and are stirred by it. We become more than ourselves when in the presence of great art because it exposes us to the transcendent. We are drawn out of ourselves in a personal response to beauty in all its forms. Collectively too, believers are given something to treasure and cherish when they are offered ecclesiastical art on a grand scale. It offers us shared cultural hopes and expectations, a collective wow-factor.

So to complete this overview we need to fast-forward a thousand years to the last century and examine another phenomenon: the death of God and decline in religious belief as a creditable entity. The reasons for this are many and varied. Being a player in the public arena, religion too has become privatized and somewhat discredited at that. It is the last thing you tell someone about yourself, rather than being taken for granted, a given. Believers do not necessarily hide what they think; they simply have a smaller place within which to express it. Churches are emptying and builders and planning regulators worry about what to do with these monuments to an age of faith. There is little money to restore old churches to past glory and even less to commission new art. So the buildings have become museums and monuments to the age of deference and belief in God. We visit them to traipse around admiring what we see rather than for the meeting with God that was promised when they were first built and adorned for the divine glory. We are invited – or even expected – to stick a contribution in a tin. Sometimes the device used to stir us to make a donation is utilitarian in the extreme, so placards warn us that it costs x number of thousands of pounds to heat the building we visit and we dutifully help pay for the heating bills – an action that is hardly designed to stir and uplift the soul, and certainly not to inspire prayer.

Beyond organized religion there are now alternatives that creep in to fill the gaps. In today's world spirituality is somehow all right, whereas religion is not; for spirituality is not branded, it does not belong to any of the churches, you can have it without being a fully paid-up member of any institution and you know it does you good. It is a pick-and-mix phenomenon, people choosing the bits they like and discarding what does not suit them. It comes packaged as a series of lifestyle choices, alluring add-ons to nurture the life of the human imagination. So people go on pilgrimage – that is to say, glamorous holidays that take them on journeys of the spirit; they fast with all the diligence of the early saints – that is to say, they diet or follow regimes or give up alcohol or cigarettes with all the rigour of the ascetics; they have their cults and saints – with football teams and celebrities directing their devotions, along with their time and money; yet they seek the beauty of holiness – that is to say, they love art.

For once again nature abhors a vacuum, and so what has crept in to replace formal religion? A return to the values of the spirit and a secular art that is all the time striving to speak to the human imagination at its most vulnerable and unwary.

All of us seek the experience of beauty and most of us would acknowledge that recognizing something beautiful is a spiritual experience. So the door is open for us to rediscover ourselves as spiritual beings through the medium of art. Art, if you like, is restored to its true vocation as a portal onto the divine. This paints a sunny picture of the relationship between religion and art, the former both respecting and protecting the latter by sponsoring artists and providing them with jobs, time, space and scriptural or historic themes for their pictures, paintings and sculptures. While this is all undoubtedly true, there is a further thread to follow, which is about the shadow side of this bright history. It is about orthodoxy, or what is 'in' and what is 'out'; what is good art and what is bad art.

When the Church was in control, it had the ultimate say in such matters. It could choose what to commission and what not to commission, such is the power of patronage. This meant that certain depictions of the human form or of sex were not acceptable but also, more importantly, that the Church had the means to enforce this orthodoxy. For not only could it withhold patronage, but it would also develop its own police, namely the inquisition and, in time, the Congregation for the Doctrine of the Faith. Heretics, those deemed to have transgressed, could be punished and destroyed.

Every orthodoxy creates goodies and baddies, insiders and outsiders. That is the name of the game. Yet what matters is how we treat the outsiders because, very often, they carry the flame of some sort of promise for the future. They can be prophets, bearers of truth for another age, so we are mistaken if we try to dispense with them or punish them for their beliefs without talking to them and trying to understand these beliefs.

Take Martin Luther, for instance: had the Church acknowledged its own corruption; had it recognized the emergence of the newly educated middle classes or bourgeoisie, who wanted to read and understand the Bible; had it any sense at all that it could no longer pretend to be the only source of grace – and hence salvation – in people's lives, then the Reformation could have been avoided. This is because Luther's concerns would have been recognized and his prophetic role admitted. And if the Reformation had been avoided like this, then the worst excesses of Puritanism too could have been restrained. Wells Cathedral would still have its full complement of art, as none of those heads would have been knocked off in the name of religion.

If you stand on holy ground, as artists do, in the presence of God, then you have another theological insight which cuts to the heart of Christian and artistic living. For you are blinded by the light of what you see and it makes everything else seem relative. If religion – and art – exist to bring us into the presence of God, then we can let go of our need to terrorize those who do not think like us and embrace them as fellow searchers, trying to respect the integrity of their consciences and their journey to God.

Art too has its orthodoxies; they are not the preserve of religious bodies. And so there is a further issue to grapple with. For much religious art is popular; that is to say, it was invented by an illiterate, peasant class. I went once to a Maundy Thursday Mass in a small village on the US border with Mexico. On the altar there stood a brown china cockerel in all his glory. He was really tacky yet he was there to remind us of the moment when Peter betrayed Jesus and the cock crowed. Elsewhere I have seen biros of the Sacred Heart, fridge magnets of Mary and car rear-window nodding popes. None of these is high art. Rather we call them tat and cover our embarrassment with a laugh. Yet without its popular manifestations, religious art would be elitist and for the few, rather than the many.

That is why I collect Santons, namely French Provençal crib figures that depict characters from a typical village – along with the usual suspects, namely Mary, Joseph and the child Jesus, the shepherds and kings. These figures wear nineteenth-century clothes and year-by-year I unpack them from their box and set them up in my sitting room, to prepare for Christmas. Over the years, I have become more inventive with them. At first they would all come devoutly to the crib on Christmas Day. The kings would be hidden in a plant pot and only arrive on January 6, the feast of the Epiphany. Nowadays I play around with them more. There are groups of villagers who are uncertain, so they turn their back on the whole event and stand around the well, discussing with each other these things 'that had come to pass'. The garlic seller is loudly debating with the postman; the man with his catch of sardines cannot quite hear what the farmer with his hand clasped firmly round a goose's neck is saying. I think the breakthrough moment when these characters began to live a life of their own came when I introduced a small pig with a curly tail onto the scene. After all, he is strictly un-kosher and I had no idea about where to put him. He could not really pretend to be a sheep and come to the manger along with the shepherds. So I put him behind the stone cypress tree, where he made common cause with a lone turkey and they could both moan about Christmas together.

All pure fantasy of course, and in questionable taste, no doubt. But I love my crib and treasure the moment when it can come out of its box and the drama of salvation can be reenacted in my own home. Popular art allows you to do that. So roll out the fridge magnets and nodding Popes and lose your inhibitions about the place of high art. Religious art, even in its popular manifestations, can help people find God in the most unexpected places.

What is art for?

In the presence of great ideas and of great art we stand on holy ground. And we need to know that that is what we are doing. That is the message that our world needs to hear. We stand on holy ground, the place of encounter between us and God, the place where art comes into its own, however humble it may be.

In my bathroom I have a painting called *Overflowing Moment*. It shows the Virgin Mary, completely naked, stepping into a deep blue bath. Above her there hovers an angel. Gabriel's wings are woven like a giant butterfly's rather than feathered like a bird's. He is bathed in a golden light that contrasts with the blue bathwater. He is clearly in motion because his hair streams up behind him and his outstretched arms hold him in balance and enable him to slow down on his trajectory so that he can deliver his message to Mary. There is an open window to the right of the picture with views onto the fields of a nearby village, called Croscombe. The annunciation comes to Somerset through the paintbrush of a gifted young artist, who just happened to be curate in that village when he painted the picture. It is full of movement and colour and light until you come to the still figure stepping into her bath. Then there is serenity and peace and acceptance of the will of God in this maiden who was 'sore afraid at the angel's salutation' as the moment flows over into hope and light for the future.

The artist is Nigel Done, whose *Light of All the Ages* features on the front cover of this book. I love the way his painting situates the incarnation in a given location; the word becomes flesh even in my bathroom.

Some exercises to help you pray with art

1 Choose a favourite picture and write a description of it, as I have just done, to help someone else try to understand what it looks like and what it means to you. Try to explore its meaning in what you write. If it is a picture hanging in your house, dust it and clean the glass carefully before you start.

2 Go back to <http://touregypt.net/featurestories/catherines2.htm> or to the images from the 'Book of Kells' at <www.snake.net/people/paul/kells> and select an unfamiliar one to use as a screensaver. Follow the instructions you are given online.

3 Where is your nearest cathedral? Go there for a visit and breathe in the atmosphere. Find a piece of art you really like and sit down in front of it to think about the artist who created it. Give thanks to God the creator for the gift of the artwork you see before you and try to learn its lessons.

9

Prayer in cyberspace

The Internet – friend or enemy of the gospel?

Prayer resources abound on the Internet. Should we be surprised that this most modern of media has become a vehicle for prayer? I think not. Yet there are those who see the world wide web as something intrinsically secular and, if anything, an enemy to the gospel and harmful to true religion. They associate it with pornography or cheap offers of Viagra or online gaming, rather than anything to do with God. In reality this is far from the truth, for the Internet is the last in a long line of tools – including pulpits and microphones and radio – that takes us back to the first description the gospel gave of spreading or broadcasting the good news, namely the parable of the sower.

There was a man, Jesus tells us in Matthew 13 (and the story appears in Mark and Luke too), who went out to sow seed. Some fell onto the path where birds of the air swept down and ate it, some fell among rocks, some into thorns and brambles, and some onto good ground, giving a crop 30, 60 or even 100 times what was originally sown. There is something reckless about the sower. He is carefree and generous as he flings handfuls of grain into the air; he trusts the Lord of the harvest (Matthew 9.38) to give him a good yield. So too with someone who trusts to the Internet such an important task as carrying the gospel message. After all, the medium is volatile, as volatile as the air into which the sower cast his seed. It relies on a connection as reliable or unreliable as the ether itself, even with broadband. Once out of the sower's hand anything can happen to the seed, yet the sower throws it with gay abandon, in the certain knowledge that some will go astray. So too with our megabytes, for there is rocky and thorny ground in cyberspace, just as there is in the average field. And even if you get a hit, there is still the inbuilt uncertainty that may mean a poor harvest, a mediocre one or even a belter. So too on the web: nothing is certain, but anything is possible.

Those who use it in the service of the gospel do so with some of the imaginative hope of the sower. They are only too aware of the dangers of cyberspace. After all, it is full of people and wherever you have people you get unpredictability and even sin. Yet type the word 'God' into any search engine and you get some 525 million hits. Type in 'prayer' and there are 99.6 million sites to visit. Combine the two and the tally drops to 2.23 million. After sex and health, religion is the third-highest player on the Internet. So what is required is discernment, to reduce these many hits to half a dozen worthwhile ones and to explore what the Internet can and cannot do to help us pray.

After all, it is not a teacher. Neither is it a moral agent. There is so much that seems possible online that occasionally we need to be reminded that the Internet cannot and will not tell us what to choose, despite the control exercised by clever search engines. In itself the web is not a person or even an agency or a conglomerate, so it cannot be painted as either morally good or morally bad without some further exploration. It is we, the people who put stuff online who are the teachers and the moral agents. The net itself is no more than a carrier – a spectacularly powerful one, admittedly, but no more than a carrier, a basket for ideas. Some of these will be crazy, some invaluable; some will be dangerous, some can transform us. The critical thing is to work out how to tell one from the other. Both those of us who put material online and those of us who go searching have to bear the responsibility for what we do when we set out into cyberspace. Just because the Internet is the biggest basket the world has ever seen, with seemingly limitless opportunities for uploading information and pictures, ideas and images into cyberspace and then downloading again into our offices and homes, its sheer size does not dwarf our capacity for making choices about what we upload and the sites we visit.

Indeed, it can be argued that the Internet increases our capacity for moral judgement because it requires personal discipline not to go looking for apparently harmless sexual stimulation or for wacky stuff about our personal health or politics, let alone our religious beliefs. The argument that, 'It's not going to hurt anyone. After all, I'm a consenting adult, alone in my own sitting room or office and I can do what I want' does not hold good. You do not have to be a prude to realize that other people have already been hurt in the production of overtly sexual images. By not looking you are strengthening the resistance to such material, reducing the client group, if only by one. By not visiting bogus quacks or mind doctors online you are limiting their power to do harm more generally.

What is the particular power of the Internet? Why is it so especially potent? It is relatively cheap, easy to use and instantly accessible. Already it seems to be everywhere; soon it really will be, with screens on our fridges and dashboards a norm, as well as on every mobile phone. Yet its real power lies in more than its universality. The combination of word and image is what gives it its energy and force. For words alone and pictures alone can only drive the thinking of half our minds. By bringing the two together, the Internet exercises an uncanny power both to suggest and to interpret and explain, all in one go.

The Internet and prayer

This uncanny power is also why the Internet is uniquely able to help us pray. For this dual input to our eyes and ears means that exercises downloaded from the web can stir our hearts and imaginations in a brand-new way. Another reason why the Internet can help us pray is that there is something congruous between spiritual realities and cyber-realities. Cyberspace exists 'somewhere else'. We have all the evidence that it is real because it appears in front of us on our computer screens. We can experience its effects and so know it exists without actually going there. That is true too of spiritual realities. In their case, we are unable to touch them or see them or taste them but they are nevertheless real and so, quite reasonably, we look for evidence of their existence in 'another place', namely in the lives of people around us.

The Internet provides us with a rich seam of metaphor. On a website such as <www.vlib.us/web/worldwideweb3d.html> you will see an image of the world that glows with light: a 'picture' of the web. The accompanying text reads,

> This illustrates in 3-D the actual domains and connections of the world wide web. Colors have been added to represent .edu, .gov, .com, etc. domains. I've always seen the web as bubbles – some large, some small – and vectors – thick or thin. This is the best graphic device I've seen to show that connectivity.
>
> (George Laughead Jr of <www.vlib.us>)

Now we know that communication is fundamental to the whole human project, whether at the level of the individual and of human community, whether on a local or on an international scale. Communications matter and connectivity is a critical human value. They make a difference to how we live with ourselves and with one another. This image from the Internet shows how transformed the world has become because of the power of the web. We are in touch with each other as never before.

There is an added consideration as well. Our world is awash with information. We risk drowning in it and are overexposed to a welter of messages which come to us from telephones, computer and TV screens, radios, cassettes and CDs, audio books, magazines, journals, junk mail, adverts, the Internet and old-fashioned print-medium books such as this even. How are we to use the media that lie within our control to sift through these messages and discern which ones we should listen to? How can we develop a theology of communications which builds on the project of trying to be human? What governs our judgement and guides our choices?

Ezekiel provides me with an image for exploring these questions. The prophet is in exile when he has a startling vision of cherubim and a fiery chariot circling over him. Then he hears a voice saying, 'Take fire from between the whirling wheels, from between the cherubim' (Ezekiel 10.6, RSV). Ezekiel's vision of the fire, the cherubim and the creatures surrounding the divine mystery is a vision of the otherness of God. The prophet's name means 'God strengthens'; the strength, in this instance, is given to Ezekiel in a place of abandonment and desolation, among the exiles by the river Chebar in Babylonia. This was a place from which a priest such as Ezekiel could be forgiven for assuming that God was absent, beyond the call of prayer, beyond the sight of the believing mind. Yet Babylon, the very antithesis of the Holy City of Jerusalem, turns out to be a place of disclosure. God is revealed even in Babylon. The house where Ezekiel stands is filled with the brightness of the glory of the Lord. How is this?

The wheels, the whirling wheels, take the divine presence everywhere. They tell us that God is everywhere and going everywhere. That God does not turn his back on us and, in the words of Psalm 27, we shall see him 'face to face'. We can only go one way at once. With God there is no such aligning of sympathies. In the movement of the whirling wheels, access is all. God comes towards us and does not turn his countenance from us. God is infinitely mobile and constantly in movement.

And there is more, because Ezekiel's vision is also of the four faces which ride upon the wheels of fire. These are of the cherub, of a man, the lion and the eagle. Mysterious images, mysteriously placed. The Church has spent 2,000 years telling us that it should be one: that there is one Lord, one faith, one God, one Church. Yet something in the Scriptures subverts the easy simplicity of this claim. The four wheels are about more than mobility; what we have here is more than a recalcitrant supermarket trolley, carrying God about on sparkling chrysolite. What we are given here is intimation that within the Godhead there is a further task, which is about communication. This text is not about a lone God, or even a lonely God who seeks out the company of Ezekiel, even in Babylon. It is about the very nature of communications within the Godhead. For where the four wheels communicate and work together, we are told something about how we are to live together.

God is a communicating God, and when we communicate we learn what it means to mirror God, who is three in one, one in three. The more diverse our communication gets, the more we approach the complexity of communications within God. Is it for this reason that the four images in Ezekiel's vision are later taken up by the Christian tradition, which uses them to depict the four evangelists? For the four Gospels are Christianity's most self-conscious attempt to tell us about God.

True communications allow for diversity and actively promote difference between us because they allow us to say who we are, truthfully. The Internet, by its very complexity and diversity, makes telling our truth possible. So the world wide web becomes a massive metaphor, both telling us about a real world beyond the known world of science and our senses and also revealing to us a whole other dimension to our understanding of God the communicator. Its density and complexity enables us to face in more directions than one and forces us to talk to each other and to try to understand each other. That is its power, bringing both a promise and a challenge.

The promise is easy to describe: with websites dedicated to giving us information about their personnel and structures, all the Christian Churches have been able to ride on the back of the information boom. We now have pictures of everyone in a parish, or diocese, along with a description of what they do, all set to smile at us from their illustrious position in cyberspace. We now know what times services are and how to get to them. All of this is great and it leads to greater information and transparency. What about the challenge? This is harder to describe: it is something about maintaining a sense of the sacred, about enabling the human spirit to breath alongside this technological giant, rather than to be overwhelmed by it. It is about not allowing ourselves to be mechanized or digitalized; in a word, remaining free and discerning and true to our spiritual identity and calling. For we are more than the size of our hard drive and the speed of our broadband connection. They are there to serve us, rather than the other way round. Human beings need to be free to be able to pray, rather than tied up in gigabytes.

'Sacred Space'

So let us examine a successful praying website and find out what makes it work. The one I have chosen is run by the Jesuits in Ireland and it has a distinctly Ignatian flavour. At <www.sacredspace.ie/en> you find an invitation: 'We invite you to make a "Sacred Space" in your day, and spend ten minutes, praying here and now, as you sit at your computer, with the help of on-screen guidance and scripture chosen specially every day.' The screen makes this offer in 22 languages, ranging from Japanese to Croatian, from English to Catalan. At the head of the screen is an image of a headland over a silvery sea, and the background wallpaper is a pale bluey grey.

Click for a brief outline and you are told,

> It might seem strange to pray at your computer, in front of a screen, especially if there are other people around you, or distracting noises. But God is everywhere, all around us, constantly

> reaching out to us, even in the most unlikely situations. When we know this, and with a bit of practice, we can pray anywhere! The following pages will guide you through a session of prayer, in six stages, including preparing your body and mind, and culminating in reflection on a scripture passage chosen specially for the day. The stages are: The Presence of God, Freedom, Consciousness, The Word, Conversation, and Conclusion. Although they are written in the first person – 'I' – the prayers are for doing, rather than for reading out. Each stage is a kind of exercise or meditation aimed at helping you get in touch with God, and God's presence in your life.

So that is the claim: how is it realized?

Each week the prayer exercises change. There is one for each day of the week, with instructions helping you draw the meaning out of a given piece of Scripture. Should you get stuck, there is even a link called 'Need inspiration?' What really makes the site work well is both the concept and the content. The concept, that it is possible to slow down and use the computer to lead you through a series of exercises, is deepened by a sympathetic use of another Internet-specific device: each image fades into another, giving the impression of a seamless garment. The content is beautifully handled because it draws out a response from the searcher. So every prayer will be unique, even while the instructions are the same in each case.

Not content with offering the prayer material online, the web designers have also taken the additional step of offering it to mobile phone users too. They say,

> 'Sacred Space' has always been accessible on the simplest of computers. It seems, however, that it has not occurred to many people that the little computer that is their phone is able to do a lot more than talk and text. Setting up a phone's browser to get to www.sacredspace.ie/mobile may deter the fainthearted, but the reward is that you can access the daily prayer wherever you are. It may help you to pray when you are in a place that is suitable to you.

> Some people find that the small screen of the digital organiser or phone is more suitable for their prayer, as they are without the ready distractions that surround the usual computer's environment.
>
> Even if you wonder how to deal with those 'No phones in church' signs, you could send someone a message, 'Take some Space – Go to www.sacredspace.ie/mobile and you're there.

The website is a winner when it comes to inspiration. What it lacks is a more subtle use of the Internet's ability to use word and image – and indeed sound – simultaneously. The artwork is minimal, but no less effective for that, and you have the feeling that you are joining a community of praying individuals. At the bottom of the homepage is a link to endorsements of the site, so a visitor can check out how it works for other people. An example: 'Thank you for this sacred space: a place to focus at the start of the day, a source of refreshment in the midst of a busy day, or a place to unwind in God's presence at the end of the day.' A counter tells us that 4,014,741 people visited the site in 2007, 500 an hour going online to pray during December alone.

For people who prefer to discover more about prayer and to do so in a community context, there is the Alpha Course website at <www.alpha.org>, which is a model of its kind. When you visit the site you are faced with a neutral question, to which Alpha has a serious answer:

> Ever wondered what it's all about? Over 2 million people in the UK and 10 million worldwide have now attended an Alpha course, an opportunity to explore the meaning of life, running in tens of thousands of churches of all denominations across the world. Alpha is an opportunity for anyone to explore the Christian faith in a relaxed setting over ten thought-provoking weekly sessions, with a day or weekend away.

A short video presents the life cycle of a modern couple on a production line. He buries his anxieties in a glass of beer; she goes shopping. They get together, marry, have children, experience further pressures from the costs of running a home, a car and so on. They have children who grow up and then themselves topple off into their coffins and die. Is there more to life than this? Yes, Alpha insists. At the foot of this first screen another video presentation shows an evening at an Alpha course. The welcome is evident – and so is the sense that this is for modern people, people like us, who have reasonable aspirations but a sense of emptiness: a God-shaped hole in their lives.

The site is commercial, in the sense that it acts as a showcase for a named product and a named – and highly successful – approach to evangelization. I particularly like the instant question box. All you have to do is give a name and type in a question: 'If God did exist, and you could ask one question, what would you ask?' Now some of these questions are frivolous or wacky; for instance, Peter says, 'where did i leave my car keys? if i become christian do i get some sort of spideysense for car keys? Thanks.' Or Mel has 'Where can I get a decent quality recording of the ENTIRE Bladerunner soundtrack?' An unknown visitor writes, 'Can I please have Nintendo Wii for Christmas?' Clearly one intended for Father Christmas there, so a wrong address. But more power to Alpha for not screening out these rogue questions, as they lighten things up.

Other enquiries are put in the spirit of the original question. So the simple word 'Why?' crops up again and again. Why evil? Why suffering? Why God? This website does not give answers; it directs the questioner towards a serious source of answers and is highly professional and works well – all qualities Alpha devotees have come to expect. For opportunities to pray with other people in a live context, this website will offer an opening to many.

The Internet and prayer resources

The Internet has many different resources to help people explore the Christian tradition of prayer. To gain a general overview of what is going on when we pray, go to <www.whathappenswhenyoupray.net>, which has been prepared at the University of Warwick. For Celtic inspiration, go to <www.faithandworship.com> or the Iona community's website at <www.iona.org.uk>, where information is available about all their Wild Goose material. For Christian contemplation, a visit to <www.johnmainprayer.com> is a must, or try the World Community for Christian Meditation at <www.wccm.org/home.asp?pagestyle=home>, which owes much to the Benedictine tradition developed by Dom John Main OSB. If you prefer to read your devotions from a book, rather than online, a list of Julian of Norwich resources is available at <www.friendsofjulian.org.uk>, or you could try any of the reputable publishing houses, such as <www.spck.org.uk/cat/index.php> or <http://www.litpress.org>, which claims to provide 'Essential Resources for a Worshipping World', for example. More everyday prayers are available at an all-singing, all-dancing website entitled <www.beliefnet.com/prayeroftheday/faith_prayers.asp?paid=68>, which has many other resources too.

Online versions of the Bible also proliferate. I regularly use <www.devotions.net/bible/00bible.htm> to locate Scripture quotations in the New Revised Standard Version. But <www.biblegateway.com> gives many different versions of the Bible in languages as diverse as Chinese and Swahili, as well as English. Or try <www.bible.com> with its daily selected readings and commentary. For a really good Biblical concordance, go to <http://bible.oneplace.com>, which comes from the USA Southern Baptist Theological Seminary. Many sites for Scripture scholarship come from the more Protestant end of the web and they bring serious resources online, as their concordances demonstrate.

The secret is to search on combinations that will meet your need, such as 'prayer and Christianity', 'meditation and Anglicanism' or 'modern worship'. In this way you will increase the quality rather than quantity of your hits. Once you have found a site, use obvious ways of checking out its suitability. If it comes from a Church or a university or theological college, you have an instant way of validating it. If it comes from an enthusiastic individual, it is important to bear that in mind while sifting through it. Type in other identifiers, such as Catholic, Protestant, Evangelical, Anglican or Quaker – to mention but a few obvious examples – to further refine your searches.

The Internet and news

Any Christian praying for the world or concerned about world events will want to have access to a good news source. The Internet is especially good at providing up-to-date information and providing stories as they break. Obvious examples here are websites such as <www.reuters.com/news/international> or <www.uk.reuters.com> or <www.bbc.co.uk> or <www.cnn.com>, but there is also a need to follow news gathering such as this with comment and analysis. Type in the name of your favourite newspaper to understand more, or for another approach altogether go to <www.thinkingfaith.org> or <www.thetablet.co.uk>, where more informed opinions from leading commentators are available. Or try the BBC's admirable Religion and Ethics links at <www.bbc.co.uk/religion> to gain more understanding of religious issues that underlie many of the world's news stories. Each of these media sites is run on a giant scale and the information is trustworthy because of this. They offer two qualities the Internet can excel at: 'currency' – that is to say, they are up to date; and authority – that is to say, they are reputable.

In the Christian tradition, prayer and almsgiving go hand in hand. We pray for other people, evidently, but we also have to put our hands in our pockets to help them out. At the website called <www.thehungersite.com> this is not difficult because what you are giving is a click of your time – which probably explains some of its popularity. The secret is to remember to do this every day, so maybe this is one to turn into a shortcut and to have on your screen as a prompt to make a daily visit. You may have your own preferred charities and wish to give directly to <www.cafod.org.uk> or <www.ChristianAid.org.uk> or <www.tearfund.org>, which even has a page dedicated to what it calls 'Current prayer news' under a button called 'Praying'. A site run by the Australian Council of Churches at <www.ncca.org.au> will carry your prayers or your money even further afield, as will its US equivalent at <www.ncccusa.org>.

Going on retreat

Another way of deepening your personal life of prayer is to go on retreat or seek some quiet time where you 'go aside' from your everyday life and find time for God elsewhere. You might want to do this as an individual or go with a group of like-minded people. To embark on such an important journey is not like joining Facebook or trying out a dating website. A much more serious intention requires serious websites. Type 'USA retreat houses' into your search engine and you will get some 222,000 hits, so refine your search, for listed here are holiday camps, yoga camps and so on. Remember to spell the word 'centre' correctly, i.e. 'center' if you want to try the combination 'America retreat center' instead. This will get you some 213,000 hits, so that is already an improvement. Refine your search by adding the word 'Christian', or even 'Catholic' and the name of your state or the state where you would like to go. The results at a site such as <www.catholicusa.com/retreat_centers/retreat_centers.htm> will give you helpful lists.

And do not forget Canada, as one of the world's most famous retreat houses is at Guelph in Ontario. The online mission statement at <www.loyolahouse.ca/main.php> describes the

Jesuit Loyola House as 'a welcoming space where men and women are dedicated to nurturing a deeper spirituality in people, leading to inner freedom and loving service'. That connection is an important one, for the aim of a good retreat is not the same as that of a self-improvement course. 'You will know them by their fruits', is the claim in Matthew 7.16, and the fruits of a sound spiritual life will be seen in greater and more loving service of others.

At <www.cathcomm.org/cathcomm/retreats/index.html> you will find a list of retreat houses in Australia helpfully listed and organized so you can visit them by region, by state and by spirituality. A Quaker website in New Zealand has a comparable list at <www.righttotheheart.com/conference/index1.htm>, along with a Christian Conference Centre Directory. In the UK a comparable list is held at <www.eden.co.uk/directory/christian_conference_centres_hotels_2.html>, while opportunities for retreats proper are given at <www.retreats.org.uk/general/links.htm>, which gives useful links, including one to the Quiet Garden Movement where individuals or groups can find space in other people's gardens. At <www.quietgarden.co.uk> you can experience the treasures of its ministry of hospitality and prayer.

So many choices and a world – and its gardens – to visit. No wonder the Internet is increasingly becoming a lifeline for people who want to pray. There is an obvious obstacle to overcome, for none of us wants to hand over access to our soul to a machine. Once you remember that the technology exists to serve you and not the other way round, then you too can launch into cyberspace with some of the joy and the expectation of the sower who went out to sow his seed.

Some exercises to help you pray while you are online

1. Go through the websites in this chapter. Choose three to mark as favourites and use them regularly over the next few days. Then choose one you will try to visit more often.
2. Go to your own parish's website. Pretend you are a stranger visiting for the first time. If there are any changes you think should be made, get in touch with the webmaster and make a case for the ideas you have had.
3. Look carefully at your screensaver. Decide if it helps you settle down to work in a peaceful, reflective way. If it does, fine; if it winds you up, resolve to change it. To help you choose, go to sites such as <www.tnpsc.com/christian.htm> or <www.heavensoft.com/s2_cd_ss_in_christ_alone.htm> or <www.1stscreensaver.com/christian.html>.

10

Prayer when you are ill

What do we mean by prayer?

Crunch time comes in anyone's prayer life when they are unwell. For when you are ill everything changes, and that goes for prayer too. This is true whether you have a bad cold, a worrying hospital appointment, whether you are facing surgery, or indeed death.

Everything changes. Worst scenario: this means that your certainties swirl around and reconfigure in ways that may make belief difficult or even impossible. You find you can no longer pray. But even moderate ill health can make prayer difficult or lead you to question its meaning. One way to deal with this is to work out what you really understand by prayer when you are well. This will mean that you are less subject to attacks from the noonday devil when it strikes. This is the name given by the early Church to the feeling of lassitude and despair that can strike us out of the blue and make us feel terrible, inert and unresponsive when facing even minor problems. A common experience when we are ill.

So what do you mean by prayer? Put simply, it is a way of turning to God. The love we experience seeks expression and, as human beings, words flow out from our hearts towards God in love and praise. Alternatively, prayer is a way of being attentive and listening to the pulse of God beating in our world, hearing God at work everywhere and in all things. Both of these active and passive ways of responding are gifts of the

Holy Spirit who is the inspiration for all our prayer. Both draw us into the life of God, as we pray with Jesus and the Father hears our prayer. Prayer is about faith, hope and charity. It begins in faith; that is to say with belief in God and a desire to know, love and serve him better. It continues in hope; that is to say with a recognition that God is mystery and that all prayer is an act of trust. It ends in charity; because true prayer will make us more loving, more caring of other people. It seeks expression in deeds. And yet when we are ill everything goes out the window, because we find we can neither speak nor listen and that virtues such as faith, hope and charity seem to vanish from our personal radars.

Yet if prayer takes us to a threshold with the divine, swirling us into the life of God, then it is something we do not do lightly. We have to let go of our preconceptions or certainty that we know what is best. Intercessory prayers, or prayers we offer when we are asking God for something specific, are not magic and God is not some kind of guru or conjurer in the sky, to be bullied or cajoled with demands or promises. Illness puts all this into sharp relief by reminding us that we are not looking for miracles when we pray. Except that we are. We do pray to feel better or to have a scan that finds nothing or for successful surgery. So how do you reconcile this kind of prayer with the words of Jesus, given in the Lord's Prayer, 'Thy will be done on earth as it is in heaven'? 'Your will be done', not mine. 'Your will.' When we pray in the face of sickness, we pray for understanding and acceptance of God's holy will.

What is God's will for us? The answers are many and varied: God's will is for us to live fully and to care for each other, whatever our capacity or incapacity. Increasingly nowadays we are also adding 'to care for our environment' to the equation as well, with the realization that our planet needs us to live responsibly too. This is as true whether you are eight or eighty. God's will for us is that we should let go of our anxieties, whether about the past or the future, casting our care onto him. This is especially hard when you are ill, so when you are really fit and well, try to develop the mindset that will lead you to pray, 'Into thy hands, O Lord, I commend my spirit', whatever your situation. God's will for us is to be attentive, so never pass up an opportunity to grow in love and mindfulness. God's will for us is particular as well, addressed to circumstances in our own lives that only we can discern and fathom.

Hospital

Nothing sorts out your attitude to prayer so effectively as a visit to hospital. My own, more than a year ago, was a revelation to me. This is what I wrote about it in the local newspaper at the time:

> Who, in their right mind, would go into hospital by choice for a five-and-a-half-hour brain operation? A team of experts performs the technique, known as Deep Brain Stimulation, to cure tremors, once a week at Frenchay Hospital in Bristol. When I first heard from the new Somerset Primary Care Trust that I could have it, I wept from a mixture of shock and joy.
>
> That was the beginning, middle and end of any tears though, because the cool and extremely professional manner of all the people who saw me at Frenchay was so completely reassuring, I had no time to feel frightened or sorry for myself.
>
> The surgeon, Professor Steven Gill, had explained what he was going to do. He would plant two electrodes below the thalamus, on the zona incerta of my brain. This is where the tremor is conducted and can be stopped. With a 94 per cent success rate, no speech problems and no instability problems, the operation looked like an attractive option.
>
> The condition I have is called essential tremor. It used to be called benign tremor, though no tremor is benign when you cannot write or hold a cup of tea without pouring half of it down yourself. A third name is familial tremor, which I prefer as my mother and grandmother had the condition, so I have known about it all my life. In fact I was not remotely surprised

when I first began to shake – aged all of 14. The school nurse used to tell me to put my hands in cold water. That was in 1961.

By 2001, a radical new treatment had been devised both for essential tremor and for the shakes associated with Parkinson's disease. The surgeon places two probes deep inside the brain, runs a tube round behind your ear to connect them to a gadget that is inserted inside your chest. Then you are given an external remote control, which allows you to choose how high or low you want the signal to your brain to be. And miraculously it works.

Or it does now I have learnt how to control it. At first I had it on too high and was waving my upper arms around like a chicken and had very slurred speech, to the alarm of my friends. These are side effects that the doctors anticipate, so nothing to worry about. The nurse designated to take care of me at Frenchay, Karen O'Sullivan, had warned me to expect them.

She took charge of me the moment I arrived at the hospital, ensuring that I understood exactly what would happen on each of the seven days I would be there. Day one was easy, admissions and finding out where to buy a card to work the phone and telly. On day two the serious work began. Early breakfast, IQ and other tests – all carefully videoed – with 'nil by mouth' until 4.30 in the afternoon when I went off for my Hannibal Lecter moment.

Under anaesthetic, a steel frame was fitted to my head and I had a series of MRI scans while the surgeons found the pathways in my brain they would penetrate the following day. When I came round I found that the steel frame had to stay on overnight so that they could use it to navigate their way round inside my head.

I was taken down to surgery the next morning, looking a tad iller by this stage. And then the miracle began. Brain surgery is tricky at the best of times, but in the hands of Professor Steven Gill and his team, it becomes an art form. The 31 stitches I could feel behind my hairline when I eventually came round that evening were like small embroidery stitches and even the gadget in my chest has only left a delicate scar.

> Two days' recovery in hospital, a day of re-education and learning how to use my hand-held remote and I was ready to go home to Wells, where kind friends made sure I made an excellent recovery. At a recent visit to Frenchay where I went for a check-up, the batteries inside my chest were adjusted so that they go off at night. So now I'm like the central heating, programmed and robotic – and also very happy with the outcome of a highly successful surgical procedure.

So much for the facts. What about the spiritual experience of having someone fiddle around inside my brain? As I see it, there were three things at stake and one clear insight. For a start, this was elective surgery, that is to say my condition was not life threatening, so I did not have to have the operation. Yet it has transformed my life and I certainly could not have written this book – for instance – without it. Meaning I could not possibly have typed so many words or found the energy to research it. After all, shaking hands use up your brainpower and leave you feeling exhausted. So, much to thank God for.

Second, and more important, I had to ask where 'I' exist. Somehow the brain feels more like sacred space than any other organ. It is where your thoughts come from – and consequently much that makes you feel individual and unique. Yet holes have now been drilled in my skull and surgical instruments inserted into my consciousness. The probes are there for the duration of my life and the little computer in my chest has to be my friend. 'I' and it – the surgery and the procedure – are now reconciled, and I have had to accept that my 'self' has not been violated, just because something intrusive has gone inside my head. Again, much to thank God for, because of the skill of the surgeon and his team. And third, the sense of wonderment that life beyond shakes is possible, that I do not have to hide my hands and avoid eating and drinking in front of other people. So my life has been restored to me and it can be fuller and more interesting than I could ever have dreamed possible. The saints have written ecstatically about the human condition and none more so than the second-century bishop St Irenaeus, who said, 'the glory of God is someone fully alive'. That is how I now feel – thank God.

What about the one clear insight? In hospital and when I came out, I could barely pray. I could barely do anything. Yet what I very soon realized was that other people were praying and doing my praying for me. The power of prayer is such that we can do it on behalf of other people and nothing is more helpful than to pray for a sick person and pray on behalf of them. They may simply not be up to it themselves.

When you see a list of the sick on your parish bulletin, they are not there for decoration. They do genuinely need your prayers, for comfort, for strength, for the courage to endure their sufferings. By praying for and with the sick, we identify with them and help them carry the burden of all they are going through. We find a new route to become one with Jesus in his sufferings. 'Christ will be in agony until the end of the world. During this time, we must not sleep', wrote the French philosopher Blaise Pascal. The reference to sleep is critical, for Jesus knew of our tendency to drop off when faced with pain. His apostles slept in the Garden of Gethsemane when he withdrew from them to pray before his passion. He said to them, 'So, could you not watch with me one hour? Watch and pray' (Matthew 26.40–41, RSV). That command still stands.

Depression

That is why it is so especially important to pray for the hidden sick, namely for those who suffer from depression. It is one of the hardest of illnesses to bear and carries untold stigma for that reason. We find it hard to be around depressed people because all the life has gone out of them. Christians are especially bad at dealing with it, as though they think an act of faith or will power should free you from its clutches and that depression is somehow culpable. Yet the early Christians, according to Acts, were known as people who loved one another, rather than as people who were endlessly cheerful.

Over the past hundred years society has developed a more loving attitude to those who suffer from mental illness, depression included. Records from my local mental hospital, a magnificent Victorian structure that was closed to patients in 1991, tells us about admissions in 1868. A table gives the 'Forms of Disorder' from which the patients suffered: 'mania (acute, ordinary and periodical), dementia, melancholia, epilepsy, delirium tremens' and so on. Then the 'Probable Causes of Disorder' are listed. These are divided into 'physical' and 'moral'. The former are fairly standard, including accidental injury, disease of the brain, hereditary disposition, intemperance and puerperal disease. Most interesting of all are the 'moral' reasons why people were admitted. They include 'ambition, destitution, disappointment, dissipation, dread of poverty, fright, grief, loss of property, love, religious excitement and bad education'. What I find striking about this list is how contemporary these conditions sound. We may have cleaned up our language so, for instance, we would not choose to name a hospital 'The Somerset County Paupers Lunatic Asylum', but society still has casualties and many of us will have been ill with 'disappointment, fright and grief'. Even more tellingly, we know about the emotional ravages caused by 'ambition, destitution, dread of poverty' and even 'love'. Most of us will have suffered from one or all of these. They are part of the human condition and the ability to feel them in fact makes us human. Nowadays we do not lock people up because they are suffering from them, but we are more tolerant of their incidence and we have developed a whole range of professional services for people who experience them.

In the Gospels, Jesus deals with the sick more compassionately than most of us would find possible. For a start, he does not avoid them. In fact they actively come to him to beg healing, and he is careful to point out that their sickness is not the result of sin in the sense of wilful wrongdoing. They are sinners because we are all sinners because we are all human. So he actively identifies himself with the care of the sick and recognizes their special vulnerability by saying, 'Those who are well have no need of a physician, but those who are sick; I have come to call not the righteous but sinners' (Mark 2.17). This is an appeal to all of us to recognize our own sinfulness; that is to say our need for God and the redemptive work of Jesus. Our deeper malaise is that we are reluctant to identify our need, so we project sinfulness onto the sick, instead of recognizing it as part of the human condition. And on the other hand Jesus is insistent. When asked if a sick man had sinned or his parents, he roundly condemns his listeners for making that particular equation.

Jesus and the sick

The story, given in John 9.1–7, is a mysterious one.

> As he walked along, he saw a man blind from birth. His disciples asked him, 'Rabbi, who sinned, this man or his parents, that he was born blind?' Jesus answered, 'Neither this man nor his parents sinned; he was born blind so that God's works might be revealed in him. We must work the works of him who sent me while it is day; night is coming when no one can work. As long as I am in the world, I am the light of the world.' When he had said this, he spat on the ground and made mud with the saliva and spread the mud on the man's eyes, saying to him, 'Go, wash in the pool of Siloam' (which means Sent). Then he went and washed and came back able to see.

The whole meaning of the man's life is made clear in his encounter with Jesus, for at that moment 'God's works' are revealed in him and to him. Just as the first man, Adam, was made from 'dust from the ground' (Genesis 2.7, RSV), so this blind man is remade with mud and spittle and 'he went and washed and came back able to see', as he became refashioned into the life of Jesus. This story works at both a symbolic or metaphorical level and also a physical one. Not everyone born blind has that much luck. For most of us our illness is not necessarily an experience of grace. That is why most of us ask questions about the existence of evil or disease and sickness in our world. We cannot fathom how a loving God could possibly allow so much to go wrong. And while those who see evil as a consequence of free will can explain away human violence or recklessness, this does not deal with the root problem. What we need to try to understand is that we are finite and that it is in our nature to perish. We are not going to last for ever, and the delicate balance of our bodies is programmed to permit death. We find that almost indefensible. Our fight against evil and sickness is part of a deeper struggle against our own mortality, and so our own humanity. For, of necessity, we are going to die.

In today's world it is extremely difficult to defend the idea of heaven. Our focus is on this world and living for today. Yet the Christian tradition has always resolutely defended the concept of eternal rest with God at the end of life on earth. At its most extreme it has even brokered access to eternal life, claiming to know who will go to heaven and who to hell. In a sense this is why heaven is discredited, because its gates seem to be policed in a particularly hostile way and are more often shut than open. Also, the idea of eternal rest is tedious to young, happy active people who cannot bear to be bored. It sounds like a poolside holiday, but without the possibility of trips and excursions, and so inevitable tedium after the first few days of bliss.

The reality is that we do not know what heaven will be like. All we have are metaphors and analogous ways of describing eternal life to each other. We are also the heirs of the conquest of space. So we no longer know where heaven is. For beyond our solar system lie other solar systems, an endless haze of stars. Our ancestors could speak confidently about heaven because there was an imaginary space in the heavens in general for a heaven in particular. They could not conceive of a state of being that did not require room, an actual space for it to occupy. So heaven had to be a real place.

Nowadays we can think of a place that does not occupy real space and funnily enough, cyberspace has helped us do this by providing an analogy that works well. Heaven is possible because it does not take up room anywhere. Heaven is something we need to be able to pray about without misgivings, so we can say the Lord's Prayer and the phrase, 'Thy will be done on earth as it is in heaven' without feeling we are using old-fashioned words that mean nothing.

In his dealings with the sick, even when he cures people, Jesus takes a long-term view. The material healing is accompanied by an invitation to 'See, you have been made well! Do not sin any more' (John 5.14). If, as I have suggested, the contrast he perceives is between those who seek salvation in God and those who look to their own righteousness for salvation, then there is further work to be done. This work is a kind of conversion, an active desire to look for safety and acceptance and a good name in a new place, namely 'in Christ', rather than in our own righteous efforts.

Death

In baptism we are buried with Christ so that we shall rise with him. Paul, in his Letter to the Romans, puts it like this,

> Do you not know that all of us who have been baptized into Christ Jesus were baptized into his death? Therefore we have been buried with him by baptism into death, so that, just as Christ was raised from the dead by the glory of the Father, so we too might walk in newness of life. (Romans 6.3–6)

When we receive the waters of baptism, we are incorporated into the life, death and resurrection of Jesus. And in heaven we shall live the life of Christ to the full.

If heaven is our true home then what about death? How can we lose our fear of it? For the reality is that we fight against it with every fibre of our beings and we rightly see the death of babies and children and young people as abhorrent. Yet some of our fear of death is exacerbated by the fact that we do not really believe in eternal life. 'This is the only life I'm ever going to have' is an expression used all too readily by even the most devout believers.

A 'good death' becomes one stoically borne, rather than one that leads the individual into the presence of God and so to the fullness of all our desires. Sceptics describe religion as a sociological construct, as something invented to help human beings cope with the ultimate anxiety, that of meaninglessness. So it is up to people who do believe in ultimate realities to prove their own point by seeking a good death; that is to say one of expectation and hope.

Nowhere is this portrayed more compellingly than by Cardinal John Henry Newman, in his *Dream of Gerontius*. The name means 'old man', so Gerontius is a generic figure, representing us all. As he lies on his bed of sickness, he prays,

> Jesu, Maria – I am near to death,
> And Thou art calling me; I know it now.
> Not by the token of this faltering breath,
> This chill at heart, this dampness on my brow, –
> (Jesu, have mercy! Mary, pray for me!)
> 'Tis this new feeling, never felt before,
> (Be with me, Lord, in my extremity!)
> That I am going, that I am no more.
> 'Tis this strange innermost abandonment,
> (Lover of souls! great God! I look to Thee,)
> This emptying out of each constituent
> And natural force, by which I come to be.
> Pray for me, O my friends; a visitant
> Is knocking his dire summons at my door,

> The like of whom, to scare me and to daunt,
> Has never, never come to me before.

The angel of death has come to summon him from the company of the friends who pray around his bed. As his spirit leaves them for the last time he is assailed by conflicting forces. Demons hover to make fun of his faith. Yet angels surround him too and they sing 'Praise to the Holiest in the Height'.

Gerontius describes what death feels like,

> That sense of ruin, which is worse than pain,
> That masterful negation and collapse
> Of all that makes me man; as though I bent
> Over the dizzy brink
> Of some sheer infinite descent;
> Or worse, as though
> Down, down for ever I was falling through
> The solid framework of created things,
> And needs must sink and sink
> Into the vast abyss. And, crueller still,
> A fierce and restless fright begins to fill
> The mansion of my soul.

Yet beyond the moment of death lies a new experience. He sings,

> I went to sleep; and now I am refreshed.
> A strange refreshment: for I feel in me
> An inexpressive lightness, and a sense
> Of freedom, as I were at length myself,
> And ne'er had been before. How still it is!

This stillness is what is promised to us all. It is something we sometimes experience when we are praying, as we hand ourselves over to God in silent contemplation and have a glimpse of what lies ahead of us. And also the 'sense of freedom' and of being more oneself than has ever been possible before. So an acceptance of humanity and, with it, the refreshment and lightness of death, of laying aside all that binds us to our anxieties and competitiveness, to the struggle of our genes for purely physical survival. Gerontius died 'in Christ' and in the hope of sharing the resurrection of Jesus. In him, as in every Christian, the promise is made plain, 'I am the resurrection and the life. Those who believe in me, even though they die, will live, and everyone who lives and believes in me will never die' (John 11.25–26).

That is a promise made to us all. Jesus is clear: even though we are to die, we will live on when we believe he is both the resurrection and the life. It is the reason why in all our praying – and especially when we are sick or dying – we come before God to lay our colours on his altar, the altar of eternal life.

Some exercises to help you pray when you are ill

1 Say the words 'God is love' over and over to yourself as an act of faith. Then shorten the prayer to 'God is' as an act of hope, and repeat it. Finally, shorten your prayer again to the simple repetition of the divine name, 'God', as an act of charity. When you are ready to, start all over again. This prayer is especially good at night.

2 Copy out the words of some of your favourite prayers or extracts from the Bible into a notebook. Use it like a recipe book to dip in and out of. Then, when or if you are ill, you will have a collection of good things to fall back on.

3 Remember to pray for other people, especially the sick and the dying. If you can manage to do this when you are ill yourself, you will be part of a great circle of light surrounding the human family at its most vulnerable. Here are the words of an anthem to help you pray.

> The Lord hath created medicines out of the earth; and he that is wise will not abhor them. And he hath giv'n men skill, that he might be honour'd in his marvellous works.